Essential Ethernet Standards: RFCs and Protocols Made Practical

Other Works in This Series

Pete Loshin, *Essential Email Standards: RFCs and Protocols Made Practical*

Pete Loshin, *Essential ATM Standards: RFCs and Protocols Made Practical*

Essential Ethernet Standards:
RFCs and Protocols
Made Practical

Pete Loshin

Wiley Computer Publishing

John Wiley & Sons, Inc.

NEW YORK · CHICHESTER · WEINHEIM · BRISBANE · SINGAPORE · TORONTO

Publisher: Robert Ipsen
Editor: Carol A. Long
Associate Editor: Kathryn A. Malm
Managing Editor: Angela Murphy
Electronic Products, Associate Editor: Mike Sosa
Text Design & Composition: Benchmark Productions, Inc.

Designations used by companies to distinguish their products are often claimed as trademarks. In all instances where John Wiley & Sons, Inc., is aware of a claim, the product names appear in initial capital or all capital letters. Readers, however, should contact the appropriate companies for more complete information regarding trademarks and registration.

This book is printed on acid-free paper. ∞

This publication is designed to provide accurate and authoritative information in regard to the subject matter covered. It is sold with the understanding that the publisher is not engaged in professional services. If professional advice or other expert assistance is required, the services of a competent professional person should be sought.

Library of Congress Cataloging-in-Publication Data:

Loshin, Peter.
    Essential Ethernet standards: RFCs and protocols made practical/Pete Loshin.
        p.   cm.
    ISBN 0-471-34596-2 (cloth)
    1. Ethernet (Local area network system). 2. Computer network protocols. I. Title.
TK5105.8.E83 L67   1999
004.6'8--dc21   99-042975
                                                        CIP

Printed in the United States of America.

10 9 8 7 6 5 4 3 2 1

Contents

Foreword

Ethernet has been around for over a quarter of a century. It started as a 3-megabit experiment running over coaxial cable, requiring all kinds of specialized hardware. It ran in a few research facilities. Today I am writing this on a laptop PC with a built-in Ethernet interface that runs at 100Mbits/second and uses common twisted-pair cabling, all available at a local computer store. In 1982, at my first employer, we developed an Ethernet adaptor for IBM S/370 mainframe computers. It was about the size of a PC. Today Ethernet interfaces are available that are the size of a credit-card. Over the past 25 years, many LAN technologies have come and gone. Each one was to be the one to replace Ethernet. Each one was better in some way. IEEE 802.5 Token Ring had deterministing behavior, which wa obviously better than Ethernet's random behavior. When Token Ring went to 16Mbits, it was faster and, obviously, faster was better. Then came FDDI, which at 100Mbits must have been better still. But Ethernet came back with 10Base-T wiring and switching, with hundred megabit, and now gigabit speeds. Gigabit Ethernet is even beginning to be used in some WAN environments over dark-fiber. Who knows.

Maybe SONET and ATM are next to fall victim. Like the pink rabbit, Ethernet just keeps on going.

But Ethernet is "just a cable." You have to run something over it. Independently but simultaneously, TCP/IP and the Internet were developed. It too started in a few research institutions. The primordial "Internet" had maybe a few dozen nodes, there was no shortage of IP Addresses, and who would have thought of charging for Domain Names (if we had even thought of Domain Names). Along with that S/370 Ethernet adaptor we built, we wrote the TCP/IP stack, and the applications and when we tried to sell the software, we'd have to explain what IP was and tell MIS people why they wanted to network their computers—and we didn't even bother to tell people about the internet. Today, it's impossible to imagine buying a computer that wasn't "Internet Ready" and TCP/IP have grown to support hundreds of millions of computers.

But with all that history and success comes a price—the historical refuse of false lore, failed protocol experiments, and bad implementations. For someone starting today, this historical refuse can obscure the essentials. The "wheat" of what's critical is lost in the "chaff" of what we once did and thought.

Essential Ethernet Standards: RFCs and Protocols Made Practical separates the wheat from the chaff. It tells you what is important and why. It also says what is not important, and why.

—Frank Kastenholz

Acknowledgments

This is where I'd normally ooze thanks effusively, citing the folks at Wiley like Carol Long, Kathryn Malm, and Angela Murphy. Yes, they helped make it happen. But it if weren't for the men and women who have devoted their careers and lives to developing Internet standards, this book—and the Internet itself—would not be possible.

Without those people—anyone who has ever contributed to a workgroup, whether by drafting a document, coding an implementation, submitting an opinion about a specification to workgroup mailing list, or attending an IETF function—none of this would have been possible. I'd like to extend my thanks to each and every one of those people.

There is one particular member of the IETF, Frank Kastenholz, who gets my special gratitude: he gave this book a good, critical look and still liked it enough to write a foreword.

Finally, I cannot write an acknowledgment section without mentioning my loving wife, Lisa, and my splendid son, Jacy. And Zoom, for whom we are all eagerly awaiting.

About the Author

Pete Loshin started writing about computers in the late 1980s for *PC Magazine* and *PC Week*, and he shortly afterward discovered TCP/IP and the Internet. Following a six-year stint as a TCP/IP network engineer for an R&D laboratory in Cambridge, MA, Pete began writing full-time. He served as technical editor for *BYTE* Magazine, as well as editor of the newsletter "Corporate Internet Strategies." His articles have appeared in magazines such as *PC World*, *Communications Week*, *Information Security*, *Data Communications*, *Communications News*, *Telecommunications*, and many others. Pete has a bunch of books about TCP/IP, the Internet, and networking, including *TCP/IP Clearly Explained* (Morgan Kaufmann, 1999), *IPv6 Clearly Explained* (Morgan Kaufmann, 1999) and *Extranet Design and Implementation* (SYBEX 1997). Pete expects to have six new titles in print during 1999. You can reach Pete at pete@loshin.com. For more information about Internet standards as well as this and any other book Pete has written, check out www.internet-standard.com.

Introduction

Standards are usually dry, inaccessible (literally and figuratively), and remote from the reality of everyday life. The Internet Request for Comments (RFC) document series includes Internet standards, but more importantly it contains the wit and wisdom of everyone who has helped to make the Internet what it is. Since 1969, engineers and non-engineers have submitted documents to this series, sometimes to document a meeting, sometimes to document a new protocol, sometimes to describe an old problem, sometimes to describe a new approach to solving that problem.

Some RFCs are more important than others, some are easier to read than others. But with the number of RFCs approaching 3,000, the one constant is that when you need to find something out about Internet standards, your best bet is to look for the appropriate RFC. Finding that document may not always be easy, but they're all in there, somewhere.

If only there were somewhere you could turn to get the gist of the standards in some particular arena; email for example, or ATM maybe, or even Ethernet.

That's why I wrote this book. First, so that anyone who needs to know more about Internet standards can find out what they need, no matter what area they are concerned with. And second, so you could have a convenient source that categorizes the standards, summarizes the important ones, and tells you where to look for all the details.

Who Should Read This Book

You need to read this book if you develop Internet applications or any network software or hardware that uses or interfaces with Ethernet networks. It will help guide you through the salient protocols, and keep you from wasting time looking at the wrong ones.

But you should also read this book if you support Internet protocols over Ethernet in any way: whether you install software that runs over and hardware that works with Ethernet or provide technical services to users of such products, understanding how the underlying protocols work will help you do your job better.

If you're involved with network administration, network security, or network design, you should read this book as well. It will help you understand how the relevant Internet protocols work and how you can administer, secure, or design your network with those protocols in mind.

Finally, if you are interested in understanding how the Internet works, whether as a college or graduate student of computer science or simply as a curious person who likes to see how things tick, you should read this book.

What's in This Book

This book is divided into two parts. In the first part, after an introduction to Ethernet and standards in Chapter 1, we get deep into the Internet standards process. Chapter 2 examines the various Internet standards and non-standards documents and discusses the different classifications that documents can fall into. Chapter 3 introduces the various Internet standards bodies, and related organizations. Chapter 4 covers the process that takes a proposed specification and turns it into a full Internet standard. Chapter 5 offers tips and techniques for locating and downloading exactly the RFC you are looking for, and some pointers to good web sites that can give you more information about RFCs and Internet standards. Chapter 6, gives some pointers to reading and interpreting RFCs. The last chapter in Part One, Chapter 7, provides an overview to the standards related to network management over the Internet and other IP networks.

The first part of the book is the introduction to the world of Internet standards; the rest of the book builds on the information in the first part, taking you through the world of Internet standards for Ethernet. Chapter 8 provides an overview to Ethernet itself, while in Chapter 9 we discuss the issues that need to be addressed by IETF standards for running IP over Ethernet. In Chapter 10 we cover the Ethernet Address Resolution Protocol (ARP), while in Chapter 11 we look at how IPv4 is run over Ethernet and in Chapter 12 we examine how IPv6 runs over Ethernet.

In Chapter 13, we look at the issues of doing multicast and broadcast transmission across Ethernet, while in Chapter 14 we discuss Ethernet and Ethernet-like network management in the framework of the Simple Network Management Protocol (SNMP) and related Management Information Bases (MIBs). Finally, Chapter 15 we consider the state of the art in IP and Ethernet standards, and give some indications of what to expect in the future for ATM and IP standards.

Internet standards continually evolve and develop over time. If something works but could be made to work better, it is likely to eventually be updated. If something doesn't work as it was expected to, it will either be updated so it will work better, or replaced by something that already does work better. This means you've got to be proactive as you study Internet standards—even as you read this book. Most of the material is based on up to date documents and discussion with members of the IETF workgroups responsible for developing new standards. The majority of the material is stable and not expected to be updated any time soon. But that does not mean it won't be updated— or that it won't be supplemented with new, complementary standards.

If you need to know this stuff, you'll need to know how to keep it all up to date. One way is to subscribe to all the workgroup mailing lists (see chapter 4). Another approach is to check out: www.Internet-Standard.com.

This is where you can go to find out the latest about Internet standards as well as get any updates or errata concerning this book. I'll be posting interesting information and news related to standards there, as it comes in.

Finally, the best part of my day is when I receive email from someone who has read one of my books. Whether you like the book or not, whether you found a typo or want to thank me for writing something useful, I welcome all reader email. So just let me know what you think of this book by sending email to me at pete@loshin.com.

I hope you enjoy reading this book as much as I enjoyed writing it.

PART

One

Internet Standards

Ethernet and the Internet grew up together. Very simply, the availability of a fast link layer network transport such as Ethernet very likely helped make the ubiquitous deployment of the Internet Protocol (IP) possible. The fact that Ethernet provides an efficient and widely supported mechanism for local area networking makes it vital to IP network implementers. One big thing Ethernet and IP have in common is their need for open standards.

As long as we all adhere to the open standards, we can all get along just fine. The first part of this book builds a foundation for understanding what Internet standards are and how they work. The second part discusses the points at which Ethernet and Internet standards intersect and how they work together.

Chapter 1 discusses why standards must be defined for IP to work over Ethernet. Chapter 2 examines Internet standards and Internet protocols. Chapter 3 explains the organizations involved in creating Internet protocols and setting Internet standards. Chapter 4 describes the processes involved in building an Internet standard. Chapter 5 provides guidance for finding Internet standards as they are described in Request for Comments (RFC) documents, and Chapter 6 explains how to read and use RFCs. Finally, Chapter 7 provides an overview to the mechanisms used for Internet network management.

Internet Standards for Ethernet

Ethernet and the Internet Protocol (IP) were practically made for each other. Ethernet provides a straightforward link layer transport; IP provides a straightforward network layer transport; and the two work together quite nicely. Despite a growth in the Ethernet standard family to include several different options for transmission speed and LAN architecture, Ethernet is widely deployed, almost universally supported, and well understood, particularly as it works with IP. We've included a brief chapter later in the book providing a general overview to Ethernet. In this chapter, we discuss why Ethernet is so important to IP and how the Internet community supports Ethernet over the Internet Protocol.

Ethernet and IP: Compare and Contrast

Figure 1.1 shows the OSI reference model of internetworking that defines seven different layers at which networks can interoperate. Although the layers can often correspond to actual discernible and discrete functions, they don't have to. Chances are good that you are

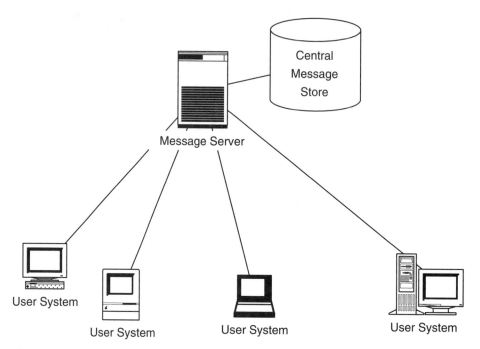

Figure 1.1   The OSI reference model.

already familiar with this model, as well as with the four-layer Internet Protocol reference model. The thing to remember about this model is that it represents how nodes on a network communicate. The application on a node can interoperate with the application on another node (or even another application on the same node). These applications "connect" at the application layer of whatever network model is being used. Likewise, when a machine is physically attached to the same physical network medium as another machine, they are linked and interoperate at the physical layer.

Rather than get into all the details about what each layer means, I've included the OSI reference model here to point out that IP and its related protocols operate at the higher layers, while Ethernet operates at the link layer. Figure 1.2 shows where IP and Ethernet are mapped on the OSI reference model.

Ethernet, in all its variations and implementations, is far from a trivial technology; however, it is certainly easier to integrate into IP internetworks than technologies such as Asynchronous Transfer Mode (ATM). Though ATM was designed initially as a telecommunications technology and only later adapted for all types of data communication, Ethernet has always been associated with data communication. As we

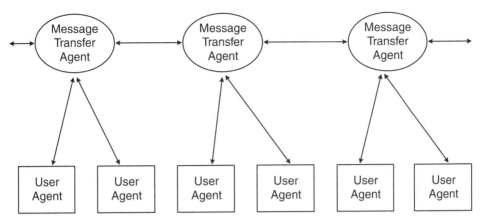

Figure 1.2   Ethernet and IP, with the OSI reference model.

see later in this book, the interface between Ethernet and IP is usually much easier to define than the interface between link layer media such as ATM and other nonbroadcast multiple access (NBMA) networks.

It is worthwhile comparing and contrasting IP with both ATM and Ethernet to get some idea of the scope of the differences and similarities. Table 1.1 lays out some of the similarities and differences and should go a long way toward explaining the relatively large number of Internet specifications devoted to making IP and ATM work together as well as the relatively smaller number of specifications devoted to making IP and Ethernet work together.

Table 1.1   IP, ATM, and Ethernet

ATTRIBUTE	IP	ETHERNET	ATM
Switched or routed?	Routed	Both	Switched
Connection oriented or connectionless?	Connectionless	Connectionless	Connection oriented
Quality of Service?	Yes, poorly understood	No	Yes, well understood
Native multicast/ broadcast support?	Yes	Yes	No
LAN or WAN?	Both	LAN	WAN
Workgroup LAN or backbone technology?	Both	Both	Backbone
Variable or fixed length protocol data units?	Variable	Variable	Fixed

What does this all mean? IP and Ethernet grew up together. To a certain extent, Ethernet and related specifications created an open standard for the physical and data link layers upon which another open standard—IP—could flourish. Broadcasts, though not encouraged for most applications, happen to be quite central to some important IP protocols and applications. Multicast is, at least for the media that can support it (such as Ethernet), an important mechanism for saving bandwidth while supporting applications such as videoconferencing. The fact that Ethernet is able to natively support multicast or broadcast makes it well suited to carry IP network traffic.

Ethernet and IP Standards

Ethernet has its own set of standards, which we touch on briefly in Chapter 8. IP also has *its* own standards. We cover those in a very general way in the rest of the first part of this book, but you could fill several bookcases with volumes describing Internet standards. In the rest of this book, we examine how the intersection of Ethernet and IP have produced Internet standards-track specifications.

Internet specifications relevant for Ethernet fall into the following broad categories:

- How to associate IP addresses with Ethernet addresses for the purpose of forwarding IP packets across local area networks
- How to encapsulate IP version 4 traffic inside Ethernet traffic
- How to encapsulate IP version 6 traffic inside Ethernet traffic
- How to handle IP multicast and broadcast transmissions over Ethernet
- How to manage Ethernet networks using SNMP

The second part of this book examines each of these categories of Internet standards and proposed standards, as described in RFC documents.

CHAPTER 2

Internet Standards and Internet Protocols

Many people consider Internet standards and Internet protocols almost magical. Although other standards may be more widely implemented, few are implemented in such a public way. Telecommunications protocols may affect more, but few standards are so interoperably implemented by so many different implementers. So what exactly makes a protocol an Internet standard? And what exactly is an Internet protocol?

As with so much else in life, these questions have two sets of answers. One set is simple, straightforward, and of limited practical usefulness. The other set, though more useful, is also far more involved. If you want the easy answers, you can find them in the next paragraph. If you want the useful answers, you'll have to read all the chapters in Part One of this book.

An Internet protocol is a set of rules that specifies interaction between networked entities over the Internet or other TCP/IP networks. A protocol becomes an Internet standard if it is listed as such in the Internet standards document known as STD-1. RFC 2500 defined current Internet standards as of its publication date: June 1999. STD-1 is published approximately once every 100 RFCs and lists the status of all current RFCs.

The complicated but useful answers require asking even more questions: What is an RFC? An STD? How are Internet protocols documented? What other kinds of documents are relevant to Internet protocols? How does a protocol differ from an application? What are the steps that must be taken to create an Internet standard? What, exactly, is a protocol? Do all RFCs describe Internet standards? Do all RFCs describe protocols? Is there a simple list of current Internet standards?

All these questions are answered in this chapter. Of course, the answers raise even more questions, which are answered in the coming chapters. Chapter 3, "Internet Standards Bodies," shows where Internet standards come from. Chapter 4, "The Internet Standards Process," examines how a protocol makes its way from being an idea to being an Internet standard. Chapter 5, "Getting the RFCs," identifies where to find documentation of current and future Internet standards. Chapter 6, "Reading the RFCs," tells you how to read and use RFCs and other related documents.

Internet Documents

The Request for Comments (RFC) represents the most important form Internet standards take and is the most often cited type of document when people speak of Internet standards. However, it is far from the only type of Internet standards-related document. RFCs represent an archive of all the wisdom of the Internet (as well as much else), from its very start in 1969.

Not all RFCs are readily available. Many early RFCs never made it into electronic format and have been lost over time. However, all the current RFCs with any relevance to the modern Internet are available online. Several different types of RFCs exist, including several special RFC series. In this section, we define the different categories of Internet documents.

RFCs

Any definition of the RFCs should start with that offered in RFC 2026, "The Internet Standards Process — Revision 3" (BCP 9):

```
Each distinct version of an Internet standards-related specification is
published as part of the "Request for Comments" (RFC) document series.
This archival series is the official publication channel for Internet
standards documents and other publications of the IESG, IAB, and
Internet community.  RFCs can be obtained from a number of Internet
hosts using anonymous FTP, gopher, World Wide Web, and other Internet
document-retrieval systems.
```

An RFC is simply a report, originally called a "Request for Comments" because researchers reported their own results, theories, and activities and solicited responses from other researchers through this mechanism. All Internet standards are published as RFCs, but not all RFCs document Internet standards. Publication of a document as an RFC may mean that it should be considered a standard, or it could simply mean that the RFC editor deemed it to be of interest or value to the Internet community.

Once published, an RFC is frozen in time. It can never be edited, updated, revised, or changed in any way. There is never any question of which is the most recent version of a particular RFC. RFC 2500, cited above, will never change, though the official protocol standards of the Internet are likely to change. Any changes will be documented in an RFC also titled "Internet Official Protocol Standards" (or something very much like that), but with a higher RFC number (probably 2600).

RFCs may be written by anyone: students, professors, researchers, employees of networking companies, employees of companies that use networking products, anyone. As long as the document has relevance for computer communications, is formatted appropriately, and submitted according to the rules (to be discussed in Chapter 4), it stands a chance of being published as an RFC.

RFCs may be reviewed prior to publication by the RFC editor, by Internet task forces, by one or more individual experts, or by anyone else the RFC editor deems appropriate, but RFCs are not technical refereed publications. When the author intends the document to specify an Internet standard, very specific steps must be taken to gain approval. These steps are detailed in Chapter 4.

STDs

The body of RFCs includes a few subsets of document series. Most important are the STDs (standards) documents. These are RFCs that document protocols that are considered to be Internet Standards with a capital S. The STD series clearly identifies the RFCs that document current Internet standards. An Internet standard protocol may have undergone several updates, revisions, or changes since it first was published as an RFC. The Internet STD series links specific protocols with static STD numbers. For example, the Simple Mail Transfer Protocol (SMTP) is an Internet standard and is described in STD-10. The most recent list of Internet standards identifies the STD-10 document as being RFC 821. Should an upgrade to SMTP be accepted as an Internet standard, STD-10 would no longer point to RFC 821, but rather to the new RFC that documents SMTP version 2 (be it called SMTP next generation or Complicated Mail Transfer Protocol, or whatever).

STDs point at the current standards and provide a point of reference for anyone looking for the most current version of Internet standards. STDs document standards rather than single protocols. A standard that comprises more than one protocol may have an STD that comprises more than one RFC. For example, STD-5 describes the standard for the Internet Protocol (IP) and it points to six different RFCs: RFC 791, RFC 950, RFC 951, RFC 919, RFC 792, and RFC 1112. These RFCs describe not only the Internet Protocol but also IP subnetting, IP broadcasting, IP broadcasting with subnets, the Internet Control Message Protocol (ICMP), and the Internet Group Multicast Protocol (IGMP), respectively.

When a specification reaches full standard status, it is assigned an STD number. When a full standard becomes obsolete, its STD number is not reused but is no longer included in the pantheon of Internet standards. For example, STD-4, "Gateway Requirements," was most recently documented in RFC 1009, "Requirements for Internet Gateways," and was phased out as a standard in RFC 1800 in 1995. In that version of the Internet Standards document, the protocol referenced by STD-4 became historic and STD-4 was retired. We come back to STD documents later in this chapter.

FYIs

In 1990, RFC 1150 "F.Y.I. on F.Y.I. Introduction to the F.Y.I. Notes" was published. The FYI documents described in RFC 1150 were intended to be a subset of the RFC document series:

```
The FYI series of notes is designed to provide Internet users with a
central repository of information about any topics which relate to
the Internet.  FYIs topics may range from historical memos on "Why it
was done this way" to answers to commonly asked operational
questions.
```

The FYI document, which is something like a cross between a primer and a FAQ, was intended to answer questions rather than to describe a specific protocol. All FYIs are RFCs, though not all RFCs are FYIs. FYIs refer to specific topics and point at RFCs, but when one RFC becomes obsolete or is replaced by another newer document, the FYI number may remain the same while it points to the newer document. FYI 1 points to RFC 1150. FYI 2 points to RFC 1470, "FYI on a Network Management

Tool Catalog: Tools for Monitoring and Debugging TCP/IP Internets and Interconnected Devices." FYI 5 points to RFC 1178, "1470—FYI on a Network Management Tool Catalog: Tools for Monitoring and Debugging TCP/IP Internets and Interconnected Devices."

BCPs

Members of another series of RFCs are called Best Current Practice (BCP) documents. RFC 1818, "Best Current Practices," describes the series as containing those documents that "best describe current practices for the Internet community." The rationale behind creating a new series of documents was that, at the time (November 1995), there were only two types of RFCs: standards track RFCs and all other RFCs.

The standards track RFCs are intended to document Internet standards, and documents are accepted into the standards track based on a very specific and rigorous process. The remaining RFCs consist of far less formal documents. These RFCs have no formal review or quality control process, which means that publication as a nonstandards track RFC affords relatively little standing for a document's content.

The Best Current Practices series provides the IETF with a mechanism to disseminate officially sanctioned technical information outside of protocol specifications. The sequence of review necessary for an RFC to be promoted to BCP status is similar to that required for an RFC to be promoted to an Internet standard, as we see in Chapter 4. While STDs describe protocols, BCPs describe other technical information that has been endorsed by the IETF.

BCPs can refer to meta-issues relating to the Internet, such as BCP 9: RFC 2026, "The Internet Standards Process—Revision 3." This document describes the process by which a protocol becomes a standard. BCPs may also refer to deployment or implementation issues, such as BCP 5: RFC 1918, "Address Allocation for Private Internets." This document provides guidelines for the efficient allocation of network addresses to avoid connectivity problems while at the same time conserving globally unique IP addresses, a depleted resource.

RTRs

RARE is the acronym for the Reseaux Associes pour la Recherche Europeenne (Association of European Research Networks). Its purpose is to create a high-quality computer communications infrastructure for Europe, using Open Systems Interconnection (OSI) protocols as well as

TCP/IP and related protocols. RARE Technical Reports (RTRs) are described in RFC 2151, "A Primer on Internet and TCP/IP Tools and Utilities" as being published as RFCs in order to promote cooperation between RARE and the Internet effort. For example, RTR 6 refers to RFC 1506, "A Tutorial on Gatewaying between X.400 and Internet Mail." RTRs often document issues related to interoperability between OSI and IP-related protocols.

Internet-Drafts

The documents that describe Internet standards as embodied in RFCs evolve over time and through many revisions before becoming RFCs, let alone Internet standards. Well before a standards-related specification is accepted as an RFC, it must start out as an Internet-Draft (I-D). As explained in RFC 2026, "The Internet Standards Process—Revision 3":

> During the development of a specification, draft versions of the document are made available for informal review and comment by placing them in the IETF's "Internet-Drafts" directory, which is replicated on a number of Internet hosts. This makes an evolving working document readily available to a wide audience, facilitating the process of review and revision.

Unlike RFCs, which are intended to survive over time, unchanged and unchanging, I-Ds are meant to be temporary. They are working documents that are meant to be replaced once updated and forgotten when no longer useful. For example, all drafts must include an expiration date, and any published I-D that is not revised or accepted as an RFC after six months is "simply removed from the Internet-Drafts directory."

While RFCs are meant to be used as references, readers are warned *not* to use I-Ds as references. They have no formal status with the IETF. They are not archived, so references to specific versions of I-Ds can not be used. Readers are warned not to refer to I-Ds in other published materials other than as being "works in progress," and they are especially cautioned not claim compliance with specific I-Ds for their products.

We discuss I-Ds in more detail, particularly as they relate to the standards process, in Chapter 4.

Internet Standards

One might easily believe that an RFC either documents or does not document an Internet standard, but it isn't quite that simple. First, a handful of fundamental standards such as STD-1 actually describe the rest of the Internet standards. Other standards in this category include the Assigned Numbers document, which lists all values that have special meaning to Internet standards, and the host and router requirements specifications.

Standards themselves have two special characteristics: *state* and *status*. A standard's state refers to its maturity level: It might be a proposed standard, a draft standard, or an actual standard. The standard's status refers to its requirements level: Is the protocol required, recommended, or elective?

The term "Internet standard" refers specifically to a protocol that is either already accepted as a full Internet standard or that is on the Internet standard track. To discover what protocols and what RFCs are standards or on the standards track, you consult STD-1. The most recent version of STD-1—RFC 2500—lists not only all the current standards, but also the RFCs documenting draft standard and proposed standard protocols as well as informational and historic protocols.

STD-1 contains lists of current STDs along with the RFCs linked to each STD. STD-1 also lists all Internet protocols by their maturity level, as described below. This document is the key to all the Internet standards: If you want to know which protocols are standards and where those standards are documented, you simply locate the current document referenced by STD-1. All other STDs are listed here.

STD-2 is the Assigned Numbers document, most recently published as RFC 1700. STD-2 includes the most important numbers to the Internet. For example, this document lists the values of well-known ports, reserved multicast addresses, or virtually any values related to TCP/IP protocols. However, RFC 1700 was published in 1994 and is seriously out of date. The Internet Assigned Numbers Authority (IANA) has been publishing these values online, at www.iana.org/numbers.html. This will probably change as the IANA is replaced by the Internet Corporation for Assigned Names and Numbers (ICANN). Both IANA and ICANN, and the transition from one to the other, are discussed in Chapter 3.

Standards can be deprecated, meaning they are no longer considered standards. For example, between publication of RFC 2400 (September 1998) and publication of RFC 2500 (June 1999), STD-3, consisting of RFC 1122 and RFC 1123, was removed from the list of standards. These documents describe precisely what is expected from TCP/IP host implementations, and are now listed as Current Applicability Statements, meaning they describe the way Internet entities should behave. As mentioned earlier, STD-4 for gateway requirements is no longer listed. The term gateway is no longer considered appropriate, and the new standard refers to IP version 4 routers. RFC 1812 replaces the chain of obsolete specifications for IPv4 routers (starting with RFC 1009, "Standards Requirements for Internet Gateways"), but the related standard, STD-4, has long been absent from the list of current standards. RFC 2500 lists RFC 1812 as a proposed standard and does not show an STD document for IPv4 router requirements. That specification may eventually be promoted to full standard status, at which point it will receive a higher STD number—or (more likely) it will be designated a Current Applicability Statement.

States: Standards Maturity Levels

STD-1 defines a series of levels describing a standard's maturity. There are six levels defined, along with suggestions for where and when they should actually be implemented:

Standard Protocol. This is a protocol that has been established as an official standard protocol for the Internet by the IESG. Standard protocols define how things should be done. In other words, if you are going to do Internet routing, you must use the Internet standard routing protocols; if you are doing Internet email, you must the Internet standards for email. There should be no problems with interoperability if the protocol is implemented.

Draft Standard Protocol. A protocol that is under active consideration by the IESG to become a Standard Protocol is considered a draft standard. Draft standard protocols are likely to eventually be made standard. Wide implementation is desirable from the point of view of the standards bodies, as this provides a broader base for evaluating the protocol. Draft standards may be modified before being accepted as standards, and implementers must be prepared to accept and incorporate those changes.

Proposed Standard Protocol. A protocol being proposed for consideration as a standard sometime in the future by the IESG is called a Proposed Standard Protocol. These protocols need to be implemented and deployed in order to test them, but they are rarely accepted as standards without revisions.

Experimental Protocol. Protocols that are being used for experimentation or that are not related to operational services are considered experimental. If you are not in the experiment, you should not implement the experimental protocol, though the experiment will probably depend on all participants' implementing the protocol. Experimental protocols can later be admitted to the standards track, at which time their maturity level would be changed.

Informational Protocol. Protocols that have been developed outside the Internet development community—for example, those developed as proprietary protocols or those developed by other standards bodies—may be documented as informational protocols. These specifications can be published as RFCs for the convenience of the Internet community. Examples already cited include the NFS protocol developed by Sun and the CyberCash payment protocol.

Historical Protocol. Historical protocols are no longer relevant, either because they have been superseded by newer versions or by newer alternative protocols or because there was not sufficient interest to advance them through the standards process. These protocols are unlikely to ever become standards.

Standards maturity levels depend on context. A group of network-specific standard protocols have been defined for link layer protocols. Obviously, STD-42, "Internet Protocol on Ethernet Networks," will not be implemented on ATM networks. Likewise, there are relatively few full-fledged standard Internet protocols (see the section "What's Standard, What's Not"); however, quite a few draft and proposed standard protocols are widely implemented in popular commercial products. For example, the very popular Dynamic Host Configuration Protocol (DHCP) is a draft standard, as is the Multipurpose Internet Mail Extensions (MIME) protocol. Furthermore, the Internet Message Access Protocol (IMAP) and the Hypertext Transfer Protocol (HTTP) are both still proposed standards.

Status: Standards Requirements Levels

Up until RFC 2400, STD-1 defined a protocol's status as its requirements level. These levels provided guidance as to whether the protocol should be implemented and included the following:

Required Protocol. Systems must implement required protocols.

Recommended Protocol. Systems should implement recommended protocols.

Elective Protocol. Systems may choose whether to implement elective protocols. However, if a system will be implementing a protocol of this type, it must implement exactly this protocol. Multiple elective protocols are often offered for general areas, such as routing or email.

Limited Use Protocol. Protocols may be limited due to the fact that they are experimental, provide limited functionality, or lack current relevance.

Not Recommended Protocol. Some protocols are considered not recommended for general use. They may have limited functionality, lack current relevance, be designed for special purposes, or be experimental.

To put the requirements levels into perspective, a system that implemented only the required protocols would probably be able to do little more than be visible on an IP network. Upper layer protocols such as the Transport Control Protocol (TCP) and the User Datagram Protocol (UDP) were recommended but not required. Such a minimal host would be able to do little more than respond to most network requests with error messages. Implementing all the recommended protocols would improve the situation to the point that such a host would be usable for most simple and typical network services. However, these distinctions have been removed as RFC 2500 defines RFCs simply by maturity level.

Internet Nonstandards

Although roughly 2,500 different RFCs have been published, most are not currently relevant to Internet standards. Some RFCs document protocols that are now obsolete, such as the Simple File Transfer Protocol (SFTP) documented in RFC 913. These protocols may once have been considered useful, but are no longer. These protocols are considered *historical protocols* because they are of interest only for historical purposes and are not intended to be implemented on current systems.

Some RFCs describe protocols that are proprietary and are considered to be *informational protocols*. These include documents such as RFC 1898, "CyberCash Credit Card Protocol Version 0.8," or RFC 1813, "NFS Version 3 Protocol Specification," which documents Sun Microsystems Inc.'s Network File System. These protocols are documented for different reasons, though usually to provide information to the community about the work being done by the owner of the protocol. For example, Sun's NFS protocol, while not an Internet standard, is certainly an important protocol and is documented so that others can write applications that are compatible with NFS.

Some RFCs are purely informational and do not document actual protocols. They may summarize meetings or describe approaches to specific networking problems taken by the author(s). Most informational RFCs are intended to provide important information or to raise important questions.

One subset of informational RFCs includes April Fool's documents, published on April 1 of each year and conforming strictly to the RFC format. For example, one of the best-known examples is RFC 1149, "A Standard for the Transmission of IP Datagrams on Avian Carriers," published April 1, 1990. The earliest example I found is RFC 748, "TELNET RANDOMLY-LOSE Option," published in 1978.

What's Standard, What's Not

The reader is directed to STD-1 for a complete survey of Internet standards, draft standards, proposed standards, and other protocols. Tables 2.1 and 2.2 list the current Internet standards and current network-specific standards, as they appear in RFC 2500.

Table 2.1   Internet Standards as Defined by RFC 2500 (STD-1)

PROTOCOL	NAME	RFC	STD
	Internet Official Protocol Standards	2500	1
	Assigned Numbers	1700	2
IP	Internet Protocol	791	5
	as amended by:--------		
	IP Subnet Extension	950	5
	IP Broadcast Datagrams	919	5
	IP Broadcast Datagrams with Subnets	922	5
ICMP	Internet Control Message Protocol	792	5
IGMP	Internet Group Multicast Protocol	1112	5

Continues

Table 2.1   Internet Standards as Defined by RFC 2500 (STD-1)   *(Continued)*

PROTOCOL	NAME	RFC	STD
UDP	User Datagram Protocol	768	6
TCP	Transmission Control Protocol	793	7
TELNET	Telnet Protocol	854,855	8
FTP	File Transfer Protocol	959	9
SMTP	Simple Mail Transfer Protocol	821	10
SMTP-SIZE	SMTP Service Ext for Message Size	1870	10
SMTP-EXT	SMTP Service Extensions	1869	10
MAIL	Format of Electronic Mail Messages	822	11
NTPV2	Network Time Protocol (Version 2)	1119	12
DOMAIN	Domain Name System	1034,1035	13
DNS-MX	Mail Routing and the Domain System	974	14
SNMP	Simple Network Management Protocol	1157	15
SMI	Structure of Management Information	1155	16
Concise-MIB	Concise MIB Definitions	1212	16
MIB-II	Management Information Base-II	1213	17
NETBIOS	NetBIOS Service Protocols	1001,1002	19
ECHO	Echo Protocol	862	20
DISCARD	Discard Protocol	863	21
CHARGEN	Character Generator Protocol	864	22
QUOTE	Quote of the Day Protocol	865	23
USERS	Active Users Protocol	866	24
DAYTIME	Daytime Protocol	867	25
TIME	Time Server Protocol	868	26
TOPT-BIN	Binary Transmission	856	27
TOPT-ECHO	Echo	857	28
TOPT-SUPP	Suppress Go Ahead	858	29
TOPT-STAT	Status	859	30
TOPT-TIM	Timing Mark	860	31
TOPT-EXTOP	Extended-Options-List	861	32

Table 2.1   *(Continued)*

PROTOCOL	NAME	RFC	STD
TFTP	Trivial File Transfer Protocol	1350	33
TP-TCP	ISO Transport Service on top of the TCP	1006	35
ETHER-MIB	Ethernet MIB	1643	50
PPP	Point-to-Point Protocol (PPP)	1661	51
PPP-HDLC	PPP in HDLC Framing	1662	51
IP-SMDS	IP Datagrams over the SMDS Service	1209	52
POP3	Post Office Protocol, Version 3	1939	53
OSPF2	Open Shortest Path First Routing V2	2328	54
IP-FR	Multiprotocol over Frame Relay	2427	55
RIP2	RIP Version 2-Carrying Additional Info.	2453	56
RIP2-APP	RIP Version 2 Protocol App. Statement	1722	57
SMIv2	Structure of Management Information v2	2578	58
CONV-MIB	Textual Conventions for SNMPv2	2579	58
CONF-MIB	Conformance Statements for SNMPv2	2580	58

Table 2.2   Network-specific Draft, Proposed, and Standard Protocols, as Defined by RFC 2500 (STD-1)

PROTOCOL	NAME	STATUS	RFC	STD
IP-ATM	Classical IP and ARP over ATM	Prop	2225	
ATM-ENCAP	Multiprotocol Encapsulation over ATM	Prop	1483	
IP-TR-MC	IP Multicast over Token-Ring LANs	Prop	1469	
IP-FDDI	Transmission of IP and ARP over FDDI Net	Std	1390	36
IP-X.25	X.25 and ISDN in the Packet Mode	Draft	1356	
ARP	Address Resolution Protocol	Std	826	37
RARP	A Reverse Address Resolution Protocol	Std	903	38
IP-ARPA	Internet Protocol on ARPANET	Std	BBN1822	39
IP-WB	Internet Protocol on Wideband Network	Std	907	40
IP-E	Internet Protocol on Ethernet Networks	Std	894	41
IP-EE	Internet Protocol on Exp. Ethernet Nets	Std	895	42

Continues

Table 2.2   Network-specific Draft, Proposed, and Standard Protocols, as Defined by RFC 2500 (STD-1) *(Continued)*

PROTOCOL	NAME	STATUS	RFC	STD
IP-IEEE	Internet Protocol on IEEE 802	Std	1042	43
IP-DC	Internet Protocol on DC Networks	Std	891	44
IP-HC	Internet Protocol on Hyperchannel	Std	1044	45
IP-ARC	Transmitting IP Traffic over ARCNET Nets	Std	1201	46
IP-SLIP	Transmission of IP over Serial Lines	Std	1055	47
IP-NETBIOS	Transmission of IP over NETBIOS	Std	1088	48
IP-IPX	Transmission of 802.2 over IPX Networks	Std	1132	49
IP-HIPPI	IP over HIPPI	Draft	2067	

Reading List

Table 2.3 contains some RFCs that elaborate on the information presented in this chapter.

For the most current assigned numbers, check out the Current Assigned Numbers Web site at www.iana.org/numbers.html.

Another good resource is the Internet Mail Consortium's (IMC) IETF Novice's Guide, at: www.imc.org/novice-ietf.html.

Table 2.3   Relevant RFCs

RFC	TITLE	DESCRIPTION
RFC 2500	Internet Official Protocol Standards	This is the current incarnation of Internet STD-1 and includes complete information about Internet standards current when the RFC was published.
RFC 1700	Assigned Numbers	This is the most recent publication of the assigned numbers document. It documents assigned numbers that were current when the RFC was published.
RFC 1150	F.Y.I. on F.Y.I.—Introduction to the F.Y.I. Notes	This RFC explains what the F.Y.I. series of documents is all about.
RFC 1818	Best Current Practices	This RFC explains the best current practices series.
RFC 2026	The Internet Standards Process—Revision 3	This RFC explains how specifications become Internet standards. We return to cover the material in this RFC in depth in Chapter 4.

Internet Standards Bodies

A regular alphabet-soup of standards bodies guide, cajole, steer, and engineer standards into existence. Learning what each group does, how each group relates to the other groups, and how the groups are involved in the standards development process will help you to understand how Internet standards work. With this understanding you will be better equipped to track the standards process and make appropriate decisions about how to use those standards in your organization and products.

Some Internet standards bodies have been documented in RFCs; others make their charters available on the Internet through their Web sites. Still other standards bodies are not, strictly speaking, part of the Internet standards process, but their work affects Internet standards in some way or other. This chapter introduces the most important players in the standards process, starting with Internet groups and followed by introductions to other important standards groups. The end of the chapter has references to relevant RFCs as well as URLs pointing to organizational Web sites.

The organizations that are involved in the Internet standards process are highly interrelated and interdependent. It is almost impossible to talk about one of them without making reference to one or more of the others. Figure 3.1 shows a simplified organizational chart that displays the relationships among the bodies that are important to the creation of Internet standards. Each of these bodies is explained in this chapter.

The IAB

The Internet Architecture Board (IAB), which was originally called the Internet Activities Board when it was first set up in 1983, did not begin publishing its activities until 1990, so much of its origins are misted by time and memory. IAB chair Brian Carpenter wrote an overview of the IAB in 1996, called "What Does the IAB Do, Anyway?" (available online at www.iab.org/connexions.html). RFC 1160, published in 1990, provides an early history and description of the IAB. The IAB charter is documented in RFC 1601. These documents form the basis of this section, which details the IAB and what it does.

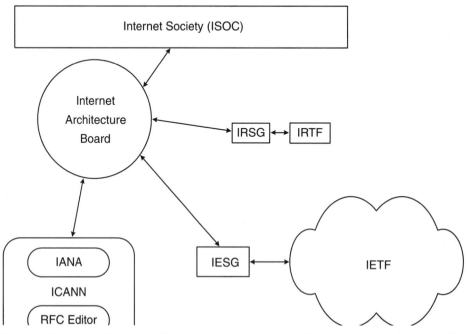

Figure 3.1 A simple organizational chart showing the links among the primary bodies involved in the development of Internet standards.

IAB History

According to RFC 1160, Internet research during the 1970s slowly grew to the point where it became necessary to form a committee that could guide development of the protocol suite. This committee was called the Internet Configuration Control Board (ICCB). In January 1983, the Defense Communications Agency declared the TCP/IP protocol suite to be the standard for the Advanced Research Projects Agency network, also known as the ARPANET. The Defense Communications Agency was the organization within the U.S. government responsible for operation of the ARPANET, which later evolved into the Internet. Later in 1983, DARPA reorganized the ICCB and renamed it the Internet Activities Board.

As of 1990, the IAB had only two important task forces—the Internet Engineering Task Force (IETF) and the Internet Research Task Force (IRTF)—both of which were established in 1986. Each task force is led by a chairman and guided by a steering group: the Internet Engineering Steering Group (IESG) for the IETF, and the Internet Research Steering Group (IRSG) for the IRTF. Most of the work of the task forces is carried out by working groups (WGs) set up for specific programs or topics.

In 1992, the IAB was reconstituted as a component of the Internet Society (ISOC), and its name was changed from the Internet Activities Board to the Internet Architecture Board. We discuss the Internet Society and the other organizational components mentioned in the charter, including the IETF, the IESG, the IRTF, and the IRSG, at greater length later in this chapter.

IAB Charter

The charter, published as RFC 1601, is a good place to start to understand what the IAB is and what function it fulfills. We begin by outlining the IAB's functions. According to RFC 1601, the IAB's responsibilities are:

1. Selection of Internet Engineering Steering Group (IESG) members. The charter calls for a fair degree of unanimity, requiring at least eight votes in favor of a successful nominee and no more than one vote against the nominee.

2. Provide architectural oversight for Internet protocols and procedures. An important function of the IAB is long-range planning. The charter calls for the IAB to track the important long-term issues relevant to the Internet and to make sure that the groups that should address the issues are made aware of those issues. The

IAB is responsible for organizing the Internet Research Task Force (IRTF) as part of its architectural oversight function.

3. Provide oversight to the Internet standards process as well as provide an appeals board for complaints about that process. The IAB, with the participation of the IESG, defines how that process is to unfold and also documents that process.

4. Manage and publish the RFC document series and administer the Internet assigned numbers. It is up to the IAB to select an RFC editor (Jonathan B. Postel, Ph.D., was RFC editor until his untimely passing in October 1998). The RFC editor is responsible for the editorial management and publication of the RFC series. According to its charter, the IAB is also responsible for designating an Internet Assigned Numbers Authority (IANA) to administer the assignment of Internet protocol numbers. Jon Postel was also responsible as the IANA, and this function will pass to the ICANN.

5. Act on behalf of the Internet Society as liaison with other organizations that are concerned with global Internet standards, technologies, and organizational issues. Some of the entities the IAB liaises with include the U.S. Federal Networking Council (FNC); various organs of the European Commission (EC); the Coordinating Committee for Intercontinental Research Networking (CCIRN); standards bodies such as the International Organization for Standardization (ISO), the International Electrotechnical Commission (IEC), and the International Telecommunication Union (ITU); and other professional societies such as the Institute of Electrical and Electronic Engineers (IEEE) and the Association for Computing Machinery (ACM).

6. Provide advice to the Internet Society, guiding the trustees and offices of the Internet Society on technologies, architecture, procedures, and, where appropriate, policy matters that relate to the Internet and related technologies. Where necessary, the IAB can call together expert panels, hold hearings, or use other methods to investigate questions or issues raised by the Internet Society.

The IAB is made up of 13 voting members, including the IETF chair and 12 full members. The IETF chair is also the IESG chair and gets a vote on all IAB actions with one exception: the approval of IESG members. Full IAB members serve for two years and are permitted to serve for any number of terms. Although IAB members may have day jobs, they must act as individuals on the board and not as representatives of any employer.

The IETF, through a nominating committee, nominates IAB members. The Internet Society Board of Trustees votes on the nominees for IAB membership. The IAB chair is voted on by the current twelve sitting IAB members. The charter states that normally six new full members are nominated each year. The charter also specifies who is eligible for the nomination committee.

How the IAB Works

The IAB usually meets about once a month through a telephone conference, according to Brian Carpenter. These meetings usually run about two hours each and are scheduled to allow members from all parts of the world to participate, though not always without some inconvenient scheduling. Physical meetings occur three times a year at IETF meetings, at which the IAB also holds an open meeting that allows any IETF member to raise issues directly with the IAB.

As we see later when we discuss the actual standards process, the IAB itself does not drive the technical work so much as oversee and guide it. This means that during IAB meetings, action is not necessarily taken on specific standards or protocols. More often, apart from the usual administrivia of reviewing action lists, the IAB attempts to strategize in depth on one or two important issues and come up with some result that can be passed along to the relevant entities: the IESG, IETF working groups, or the public, though an RFC.

Carpenter gives some examples of issues that were raised during IAB meetings held during the second half of 1995, including:

- The future of Internet addressing
- Architectural principles of the Internet
- Future goals and directions for the IETF
- Management of top-level domains in the Domain Name System
- Registration of MIME types
- International character sets
- Charging for addresses
- Tools needed for renumbering

Rather than attempting to come up with solutions to the issues that are raised, the IAB's aim is either to get the IESG to take action or to stimulate the IETF community to address the issues. When the IAB publishes RFCs or Internet-Drafts, they are in the form of statements or viewpoints rather than actual proposals for new or modified standards.

The IAB can also initiate workshops or panels that operate outside the standards process but that are intended to incubate ideas in specific areas. Carpenter cites workshops held on security, which is documented in RFC 1636, and on information infrastructure, which is documented in RFC 1862. The IAB may also initiate the formation of research groups under the aegis of the IRTF. However, the research groups are not intended to generate standards-track proposals, unlike the workshops or panels research groups, which are intended to persist over time.

According to Carpenter, in between meetings, IAB members keep track of relevant IETF and IESG activities through email lists and by commenting on draft charters of new working groups, reviewing documents that are in the last stages of getting approval, and generally helping out when difficulties arise with working groups.

Carpenter makes clear also what the IAB is not: The IETF is the standards body, the IAB is drawn from the IETF. The IAB is mostly an advisory board and has minimal input to policy issues for the Internet. The IAB might decide it is important that work be done on some kind of standard, but it can not specify where and whether that standard must be applied. In practice, though, the boundaries between the IETF, the IESG, and the IAB are blurred, and those borders are not strictly patrolled but rather used as guidelines for action.

The Internet Society

The Internet Society, also known as ISOC, was announced in 1991 and born as an organization in January 1992. It is "the international organization for global cooperation and coordination for the Internet and its internetworking technologies and applications," according to the FAQ page on the ISOC Web site. It is a not-for-profit organization with tax-deductible status based in Reston, Virginia.

Though it boasts a membership of individuals and organizations representing all segments of the global Internet community, as of early 1999 it claimed only about 7,000 members worldwide. ISOC's mission statement is "To assure the beneficial, open evolution of the global

Internet and its related internetworking technologies through leadership in standards, issues, and education." The Internet Society mission continues:

> Since 1992, the Internet Society has served as the international organization for global coordination and cooperation on the Internet, promoting and maintaining a broad spectrum of activities focused on the Internet's development, availability, and associated technologies.

The Internet Society acts not only as a global clearinghouse for Internet information and education but also as a facilitator and coordinator of Internet-related initiatives around the world. Through its annual International Networking (INET) conference and other sponsored events, developing-country training workshops, tutorials, statistical and market research, publications, public policy and trade activities, regional and local chapters, standardization activities, committees, and an international secretariat, the Internet Society serves the needs of the growing global Internet community. From commerce to education to social issues, its goal is to enhance the availability and utility of the Internet on the widest possible scale.

In terms of the number of individuals and organizations affected, the Internet Society's most important activities are those related to Internet standards. The Internet Society was founded, in part, to provide an ongoing source of organizational and financial support for the IETF and other related bodies. By the early 1990s, it was apparent that the involvement of the U.S. government as the primary supporter of Internet activities could not be sustained. To grow, the Internet had to move from being a research and academic tool to being a medium for commercial development, and it was clear that the U.S. government would eventually stop funding the Internet. In addition to funding the IAB, IETF, and other related groups, the Internet Society's board of directors, consisting of 15 Internet deities, is responsible for approving IAB members that have been nominated by the IETF nominating committee. Chapter 4, "The Internet Standards Process," outlines how the Internet Society participates in the Internet standards process.

The IETF and IESG

It may seem that the IETF would be a formal organization with membership lists, formal structure, and activities. However, this is not the case. As is explained in RFC 1718, "The Tao of the IETF," the IETF is open to anyone who shows up. According to RFC 1718, the "Internet Engineering Task Force is a loosely self-organized group of people who make technical and other contributions to the engineering and evolution of the Internet and its technologies." You can participate at any of the three yearly meetings in person, or you can participate through IETF working groups and their mailing lists.

The individuals who participate in the IETF include network designers, operators, vendors, researchers, and anyone else with an interest in the development of the Internet and its protocols and architecture. Within the IETF, most of the work is accomplished in working groups, which are categorized into different areas. We return to how working groups actually work in Chapter 4, but these are the IETF areas:

Applications Area includes working groups that address applications—in other words, anything that provides some benefit to end users—and excludes anything related to security, networks, transport protocols, or administration and management. Examples of working groups in this area include the Hypertext Transfer Protocol (HTTP), calendaring and scheduling, Internet fax, and others.

General Area currently includes only two working groups, the Policy Framework working group and the Process for Organization of Internet Standards working group. These groups address general areas of interest to the IETF.

Internet Area includes groups working on issues related directly to the Internet Protocol (IP), including groups working on implementing IP over different data link layer protocols as well as IPng (IP, next generation, now known as IPv6) and others.

Operations and Management Area working groups address issues related to the way things work on the Internet. Working groups in this area include a benchmarking group, a group working on year 2000 issues, groups working on network management protocols, and others.

Routing Area working groups focus on issues related to routing in the Internet. Working groups address multicast routing issues, quality of service routing issues, and others.

Security Area working groups focus on providing security to the protocols that other IETF groups are working on. Important working groups in this area include those addressing the IP security architecture (IPsec), groups working on various aspects of authentication, groups working on encryption issues, groups working on development of secure applications, and others.

Transport Area working groups focus on issues related to transport protocols as well as related protocols. For example, working groups include differentiated services, multicast address allocation, TCP implementation, and others.

User Services Area working groups focus on issues related to improving the quality of information available to Internet users and to developing programs that may be helpful to users. The three current working groups in this area are the Responsible Use of the Network group, the Site Security Handbook group, and the User Services group.

Most of these areas have a dozen or so working groups, and altogether there are well over 100 IETF working groups. Each IETF area has one or two area directors, who oversee and coordinate the activities of the workgroups in their areas. Each working group has one or two chairs, as well as an area advisor (usually one of the area directors).

Although the IETF can be a diffuse and somewhat nebulous organization, the Internet Engineering Steering Group is more explicitly and narrowly defined. The IETF area directors plus the IETF chair make up the IESG. Although all Internet protocol development work is done at the working group level, once the working groups are finished, it is the IESG that must approve the standard protocol specifications (or other documents) for publication as RFCs.

The Internet Research Task Force and Internet Research Steering Group

The Internet Research Task Force (IRTF) and the Internet Research Steering Group (IRSG) are not nearly as well known as the IETF and IESG. This is, in part, because the results of the IRTF research groups tend to be used as the basis for engineering work done by the IETF. Thus, while the results of the work done by IETF working groups may be enshrined as Internet standards, the results of the work done by IRTF research groups more often are used as one of many sources for new work by the IETF working groups.

The IRTF mission, stated on the IRTF Web page (www.irtf.org), is "To promote research of importance to the evolution of the future Internet by creating focused, long-term and small research groups working on topics related to Internet protocols, applications, architecture and technology." The activities of the IRTF research groups are thus more forward-looking than those of the IETF working groups: Their results may be published in peer-reviewed academic journals as well as in informational RFCs. An important difference between the IRTF research groups and IETF working groups is that membership in research groups is not necessarily open to all interested parties.

IRTF research groups currently include the following:

The End-to-End research group is concerned with issues related to end-to-end services and protocols, with particular attention to performance, traffic control, scheduling, protocol framing, efficient protocol implementations, high-performance host interfaces, and others.

The Information Infrastructure Architecture research group is concerned with developing an interoperable framework for the Internet's information architecture. Membership in this group is by invitation only.

The Internet Resource Discovery research group's mission is to develop a model by which resources can be described on the Internet. This includes the design of entities that can act on behalf of electronic resources for the purposes of indexing, querying, and retrieving information; building mechanisms that can create, maintain, and use data for those entities; and setting requirements for systems that use these entities. Membership in this group is by invitation only.

The Routing research group works on routing issues that have relevance to the Internet but that are not yet mature enough to be incorporated into work being done by IETF routing working groups. Some of the topics set forth in this group's charter include work on quality of service (QoS) routing, scalable multicast routing, routing protocol stability, and extremely dynamic routing. According to the charter, this group has a limited core membership but occasionally holds open meetings to solicit input from the rest of the community.

The Services Management research group works on issues related to the concept of "service management." Basing their work on the assumption that network management and system management are converging toward a single function, called service management, this group is investigating how best to go about creating new architectures and protocols that would allow a system/network manager to manage all different types of connected devices—from PDAs to mainframes—with the same conceptual framework and the same tool or tools. Membership in this group is by invitation only.

The Reliable Multicast research group, presumably, will be concerned with issues related to building a framework for doing multicasting reliably. However, the group's charter has not yet been published.

The Internet Research Steering Group (IRSG) membership is, like the IESG, limited to the chairs of all the research groups as well as the IRTF chair. Other prominent members of the community may be invited to serve as members of the IRSG.

Although some of these research groups maintain mailing lists or Web sites, some appear to be moribund. The address given for subscribing to the Internet Resource Discovery group mailing list is no longer valid, and other groups' mailing lists are sparsely attended. In fact, the Privacy and Security group is included on the IRTF Web site, but the group was disbanded in early 1998 because much of the group's work was done. The charter describes work that eventually resulted in the IP Security Architecture, a set of standards that have already been published in two versions as RFCs.

Internet Assigned Numbers Authority and Internet Corporation for Assigned Names and Numbers

As far as this book is concerned, the most important function of the Internet Assigned Numbers Authority (IANA) is to administer and publish numbers that are related to Internet standards. For example, if you want to know what different values in the IP header's protocol field represent, you would consult the IANA. Any arbitrary values related to Internet protocols and parameters must be assigned through the mediation of the IANA. You may not simply choose some value and then publish it as a standard. This goes for protocol parameters as well as well-known port numbers for transport layer protocols and any other number related to a protocol or an Internet standard.

However, as mentioned in Chapter 2, "Internet Standards and Internet Protocols" the IANA is in the process of being replaced by the Internet Corporation for Assigned Names and Numbers (ICANN). The need for a transition was apparent by 1996, when discussions and proposals began over how best to convert the U.S. government-funded IANA into an organization that could satisfactorily serve a global commercial Internet. Not only is the IANA responsible for protocol parameters, but it is also tasked with administering the assignment of globally unique Internet network addresses and domain names.

Internet addresses and domain names have a commercial component, as they are viewed as limited resources. There are only seven root-level three-letter domains (.gov, .mil, .edu, .int, .net, .org, and .com). Only three of these are generally available to businesses and organizations (.net, .org, and .com). There are issues relating to the way protected corporate trade names are allowed to be registered, as well as concern that additional root-level domains should be added. As for Internet network addresses, experts have been predicting since the late 1980s that the current version of IP (IPv4) does not provide a sufficiently large address space to support the continued growth of the Internet for many more years. These numbers are allocated through regional registries and are becoming more and more scarce.

After considerable debate and much revising, the ICANN proposal was accepted in late 1998—just a month and a half after Postel's death. The U.S. government acknowledged in a memorandum of understanding, dated November 25, 1998, that ICANN would be set up as a private, nonprofit corporation to administer policy for the Internet Name and Address System. The most visible and politically sensitive issues were the way addresses and domains are assigned, but the administration of protocol parameters will also be transferred to the ICANN because it was also part of the IANA's original charter.

Exactly how that function will be performed is yet to be seen. ICANN may simply continue to publish the assigned numbers online in the same way the IANA has been. In fact, by summer of 1999, ICANN's future, scope, form, and function were still unclear. ICANN funding was far from certain, and its precise duties were still undefined as were the ways in which it would interact with the Internet Society and the IETF.

More details are available at the IANA and ICANN Web sites for updates or subscribe to the ICANN-announce mailing list by sending a message to:

```
majordomo@icann.org
```

The message should have no subject line and the following command as the message body:

```
subscribe icann-announce
```

Other Relevant Bodies

Many more standards relate to networking and the Internet than those specified by the bodies described so far. Four of the most important other standards bodies are the World Wide Web Consortium (W3C), the International Telecommunication Union (ITU), the Institute of Electrical and Electronics Engineers (IEEE), and the National Institute of Standards and Technology. These bodies are profiled briefly below.

W3C

The World Wide Web Consortium (W3C) is the newest of the related standards bodies, founded in 1994 to promote the World Wide Web and help it achieve its full potential through the development of common and interoperable protocols. However, to the extent that work on important Internet protocols like Hypertext Transfer Protocol (HTTP) and the Universal Resource Identifier (URI) is done in partnership with the IETF, the W3C is most closely related to Internet standards.

Unlike the IETF, which is a wide-open organization, the W3C is an industry consortium. Individuals may join, but they must pay the full annual fee of $5,000, which is charged to affiliate organizational members (full members pay $50,000 each year). Unlike the IETF, when members suggest programs within the W3C, they must also back up the program proposal with funding for the work.

Operating out of the Laboratory for Computer Science at MIT, the W3C's members often are current or former contributors to Internet standards through the IETF. The two organizations share the goal of building interoperable protocols that foster connectivity without regard to nationality, corporate affiliation, or any other restrictive notions.

The W3C is organized into four different domains: User Interface, Technology & Society, Architecture, and the Web Accessibility Initiative. Each domain is responsible for different activity areas, resulting in an organization similar to that of the IETF areas and working groups.

The User Interface domain activity areas address issues that include data representations through the Hypertext Markup Language (HTML), stylesheets, fonts, internationalization, and others.

The Technology & Society domain activity areas address issues that include legal and social implications of the web, in particular electronic commerce, privacy concerns, digital signatures, and others.

The Architecture domain activity areas concern themselves with issues relating to the way the Web operates. Activity areas are devoted to issues like HTTP, structured document interchange using the Extensible Markup Language (XML), Synchronized Multimedia (SMIL), and others.

The Web Accessibility Initiative domain is chartered to pursue a high degree of usability for people with disabilities, through improved technology, guidelines, tools, education, and research.

As an industry consortium whose members are almost exclusively organizations, the W3C standards process is less open than that of the IETF, though interested readers will find the process document at www.w3.org/Consortium/Process/. W3C standards start out as Working Drafts and proceed to the status of Proposed Recommendations and finally Recommendations after passing through all review stages described in the process document. There are two other types of W3C documents, called Notes and Submissions. A Note is a document that the W3C publishes because it may be of interest to the community. Publication as a Note does not imply that the W3C endorses the document. W3C Submissions permit members to publish ideas or technologies for the consortium's consideration. Although the Notes are chosen by the W3C for publication, Submissions that are submitted with all support materials in order will be published. However, Submissions have no official status as W3C standards.

Because the IETF and the W3C share some of the same concerns, a high degree of cross-pollination goes on between the two organizations. Anyone interested in protocols related to the World Wide Web will find standards and protocols through both organizations. Where overlap occurs, the two organizations cooperate in the interests of interoperability.

IEEE

The Institute of Electrical and Electronics Engineers (IEEE) is an international professional organization for engineers. Founded in 1884, the IEEE standards groups work on specifications for all types of engineering pursuits including networking. In particular, IEEE standards are used to define the way data is transmitted across network media like ethernet. Important standards include the IEEE 802 LAN/MAN standards relating to ethernet transmissions, the IEEE P1394.1 high-performance serial bus bridge standards, and the IEEE P1363 standards for public-key cryptography.

ITU

With roots going back to the 1865 founding of the International Telegraph Union, the International Telecommunication Union (ITU) is one of the oldest standards bodies around. In 1947, it became an agency of the United Nations and is based in Geneva, Switzerland. Initially, it was set up to foster international standards for telegraphy, technical standards as well as standards for operations, tariffs, and telecommunications accounting practices. The ITU has evolved over the years to accommodate changes in the telecommunications industries it serves. Its activities include work on all sorts of data transmission media, including satellite, radio, and more traditional cabled transmission.

As telecommunications organizations increasingly rely on IP networks to carry voice as well as data, the ITU will expand its Internet-related activities. RFC 2436 addresses issues of interaction between the ITU and the IETF. The ITU currently has several study groups working on IP-related issues, including multimedia services and systems, telecommunication management networks and network maintenance, and signaling requirements and protocols for network media like ISDN. Other standards are developed through ITU, in particular the X.400 standards relating to message handling and the X.500 standards relating to directory services.

NIST

The National Institute of Standards and Technology (NIST) is an agency of the U.S. Department of Commerce's Technology Administration whose mission is to promote U.S. economic growth by working with industry to develop and apply technology, measurements, and standards. NIST is active in a number of important areas relating to the Internet, including standards for encryption such as the Data Encryption Standard (DES) and selection of a replacement for DES, known as the Advanced Encryption Standard (AES). NIST is also active in working on new protocols for broadband data transmission across high-speed networks including ATM, as well as research on technologies to support the next-generation Internet.

Reading List

RFC 2028, "The Organizations Involved in the IETF Standards Process," is a good place to start if you're interested in reading more. Table 3.1 includes Web sites for the organizations described in RFC 2028 as well as many others of relevance to the Internet standards process.

Table 3.1   Organizations Involved in the Internet Standards Process

ORGANIZATION	URL
The Internet Society (ISOC)	www.isoc.org
The Internet Corporation for Assigned Names and Numbers (ICANN)	www.icann.org
The Internet Assigned Numbers Authority (IANA)	www.iana.org/index2.html
The IANA Protocol Numbers and Assignment Services page	www.iana.org/numbers.html
The Internet Engineering Task Force (IETF)	www.ietf.org
The Internet Research Task Force (IRTF)	www.irtf.org
The Internet Engineering Steering Group (IESG)	www.ietf.org/iesg.html
The Internet Architecture Board (IAB)	www.iab.org/iab/
The World Wide Web Consortium (W3C)	www.w3c.org/
The International Telecommunication Union (ITU)	www.itu.int/
The Institute of Electrical and Electronics Engineers (IEEE)	www.ieee.org/
The IEEE Standards site	http://standards.ieee.org/

The Internet Standards Process

We've discussed what an Internet standard is in Chapter 2, "Internet Standards and Internet Protocols," and what organizations participate in the creation of Internet standards in Chapter 3, "Internet Standards Bodies." In this chapter, we look at the process by which a protocol becomes an Internet standard protocol. Working from two RFCs that describe the standards process and provide guidelines for IETF working groups, we introduce the activities necessary to create an Internet standard. In the last part of this chapter, we examine the instructions to RFC authors to better understand how those documents are structured and what information those documents contain.

The Standards Process

The abstract of RFC 2026, "The Internet Standards Process—Revision 3," reads:

    This memo documents the process used by the Internet community for
    the standardization of protocols and procedures. It defines the
    stages in the standardization process, the requirements for moving a

```
document between stages and the types of documents used during this
process.  It also addresses the intellectual property rights and
copyright issues associated with the standards process.
```

This RFC is currently defined as BCP-9, documenting the best current practices for defining Internet standards. The actual procedures required to turn a protocol into a standard are defined here. The document notes that specifications developed through the actions of the IAB and IETF are usually revised before becoming standards. However, specifications that have been defined by outside bodies may go through the same approval process that home-grown standards do, but the outside standards are not revised. In these cases, the Internet standards process is used to affirm it as a standard and to determine how it should be applied to the Internet, rather than to modify the specification being taken.

RFC 2026 defines the Internet standard, pointing out that the specification must be stable and well understood and must be competent technically. It should also have been implemented by more than one independent group, and all those implementations should be interoperable. There should be "substantial operational experience" with the standard, and the standard should enjoy "significant public support." Furthermore, it should be "recognizably useful in some or all parts of the Internet."

In a perfect world, the Internet standard process would be straightforward: Someone proposes a new protocol or process, people work on it over time, the Internet community provides feedback as the standard is gradually improved until the community determines that the specification is stable, competent, interoperable, supported, and is "recognizably useful." However, in practice, the difference between theory and practice is far greater than the difference between theory and practice, in theory. Defining Internet standards can be a messy process.

Standards Actions

As RFC 2026 makes clear, Internet *standards actions* must all be approved by the IESG, and standards actions include anything that modifies the state of the specification as it relates to the standards process. Anything that changes the state of a specification is a standards action. Actions occur when a specification enters the standards track, when it changes its maturity level within the standards track, or when it is removed from the standards track. None of those things can happen unless the IESG approves it.

The IESG follows guidelines devised to identify specifications that are ripe for a standard action, but the documented criteria are not hard-and-fast rules but rather guidelines. These guidelines will be discussed later. The IESG, as a group, uses its own judgment when deciding on standards actions. It has the power to deny an action to a specification that otherwise might appear to fulfill all requirements or to approve an action for a specification that might appear to fall short in one or more areas. If any parties believe that a standard action was granted or denied in error, they can resort to the dispute resolution procedures discussed later in this section.

The first step in the standards process is the entity sponsoring the specification publishing it as an Internet-Draft (I-D). Normally, this entity is the IETF working group, but it may also be an individual or some other organization. I-Ds produced by individuals or groups not directly connected to an IETF working group can be published as standards-track RFCs and are frequently published as informational RFCs as well. I-Ds are subject to modification based on community review, are transient documents, and are not intended to be referenced in the same way that RFCs are. I-Ds expire if they have not been modified for six months, though the timer starts again when a new version is published. An I-D published on January 1, 2001 would expire after June 30, 2001 if it was not revised; if a revision is published on June 1, 2001, then it is due to expire after November 30, 2001. If a revision is published January 15, 2001, then that I-D expires after July 15, 2001.

However, the whole point of publishing an I-D is to have it accepted to the Standards Track rather than to have it persist as an I-D. This is the first standards action that must occur in the standards process for any specification. No action can occur until the I-D has been available online for at least two weeks. This time is to be used for community review, allowing members of the IETF and the rest of the world to read the draft and make comments on it.

Although the IESG can't take any action until at least two weeks after the I-D is published, nothing happens unless the IETF working group makes a recommendation to its area director. It can take quite some time and several revisions before the working group makes that recommendation. Normally, one or several members of a working group write a preliminary draft of the specification and publish it as an I-D. That draft stimulates discussion within the working group, which may result in modifications to the draft. A second I-D is published, stimulating further discussion, which in turn results in further modifications. For successful specifications, this process continues until the group is able to agree that the current version of the draft is ready to be published as an RFC.

Not all I-Ds become RFCs, however. Some may languish due to lack of interest. Others may be dropped when some other specification appears to solve the problem better. Some never achieve a stable form.

When the IESG receives a recommendation for a standards action, it may consult with experts to review the recommendation. When the IESG is reviewing a document, it issues a *last call* notification to the IETF through the IETF-announce mailing list. Anyone may subscribe to this mailing list, and anyone may submit comments on the specification being reviewed. Once the specification is received from the working group, the last call period must be at least two weeks, but the IESG has the option of extending the last call period if it deems it necessary.

Although the IETF working group's recommendation carries weight with the IESG, it is far from binding. The IESG can even decide to consider a standards action different from that requested by the working group. Once the last call period is over, the IESG makes its decision and announces it through the IETF announce mailing list. If approved, the IESG then notifies the RFC Editor that the I-D should be withdrawn and republished as an RFC.

The Standards Track

Each time a specification is promoted to one of the three maturity levels of the Internet standards track—proposed standard, draft standard, and standard—it must go through the IESG approval process noted previously. This section examines the stated criteria for promotion to each level as described in RFC 2026. Specifications must remain at the proposed and draft standard maturity levels for minimum periods of time, but these minimums are precisely that: absolute minimums. Advancement along the standards track can be quite slow. Rather than quickly advance a specification, the IESG and IETF working groups prefer that the standard is correct rather than risk enshrining a flawed standard.

It is not uncommon for a proposed or draft standard to fail to advance on the standards track but to remain important for the Internet. For example, the Boot Protocol (BOOTP), documented in RFC 951 in 1985, is still a draft standard in 1999. Likewise, the IP Security Architecture, documented in RFC 2401 in November 1998, is still a proposed standard even though it replaces an earlier standards-track version documented by RFC 1825, published in 1995. When a specification stalls at some point in the standards track for two years, the IESG reviews the specification every year. The IESG may subsequently decide to terminate the effort or else decide that development of the specification should continue. At the same time, the IESG may determine that the specification itself is no longer relevant and should be reclassified as a historical RFC rather than a standard-track specification.

As specifications advance, they are usually modified. These modifications usually require the publication of new RFCs to document the new versions of the specification. Though it may not be necessary to republish a specification when it changes maturity level (that is, the specification is unchanged), in most cases when a specification advances, a new RFC is published to reflect changes. If the modifications made during the revision process are sufficiently extensive, the IESG can decide the specification should go back and restart the process.

Proposed Standard

According to RFC 2026, to become a proposed standard, a specification "is generally stable, has resolved known design choices, is believed to be well-understood, has received significant community review, and appears to enjoy enough community interest to be considered valuable." However, more experience with the specification might prove otherwise—the specification might not be valuable, or have support, be well-understood, or even stable—in which case the specification could lose its status as a proposed standard.

No operational experience or even an implementation is necessary for a specification to achieve the proposed standard level, though both of those are helpful to a specification's cause. If the specification is likely to have a significant impact on the Internet as it exists now, the IESG will very likely require that the specification be implemented and deployed.

Proposed standards are to be considered immature, but RFC 2026 encourages implementers to use the specification to build up a body of experience that can be drawn upon to judge the protocol's value.

A specification must spend at least six months as a draft standard before it can advance along the standards track.

Draft Standard

"A specification from which at least two independent and interoperable implementations from different code bases have been developed, and for which sufficient successful operational experience has been obtained, may be elevated to the 'Draft Standard' level." That's how RFC 2026 puts it. Interoperable means that the implementations are "functionally equivalent or interchangeable." To qualify, the implementations have to implement the entire specification. If some functions or options are left out, the implementation doesn't count, unless the things that were left out of the implementations are also taken out of the specification.

Where a proposed standard should be generally stable, draft standard specifications "must be well-understood and known to be quite stable." It is up to the working group chair to document the specification's implementations, as well as to document interoperability test results and function/option support test results as a part of the chair's recommendation for moving the proposed standard to draft standard status.

Once a specification achieves draft standard status, it stays there for at least four months. This period must include an IETF meeting, so this period may be extended if the next IETF meeting occurs more than four months from the date the specification achieves draft standard.

Once a specification attains the draft standard maturity level, it is considered a final specification, one that implementers are encouraged to deploy in production systems. Although the draft standard specification may be subject to changes before attaining full standard status, those changes are most likely to be limited to fixes for specific problems arising from continued experience with the specification.

Internet Standard

According to RFC 2026, Internet standard status is reserved for specifications with "significant implementation and successful operational experience." Standards are differentiated from other maturity levels by "a high degree of technical maturity and by a generally held belief that the specified protocol or service provides significant benefit to the Internet community."

Once a specification is approved as a standard, it is assigned an STD number (see Chapter 3). Most specifications have yet to reach standard level; as of early 1999, only 56 STD numbers have ever been assigned out of almost 2,500 RFCs published.

Revising or Retiring Existing Standards

What happens when an existing standard must be updated? The process is the same for a revision to an existing standard as for a new standard. Consider the case of IPv6, the revision to the current version of the Internet Protocol, IPv4 (see also *IPv6 Clearly Explained*, Morgan Kaufman 1999). Work on the revision began in the IPng working group in the early 1990s, with the first series of IPv6 standards-track RFCs published in 1996. Continued work resulted in new versions of the IPv6 specifications, published in RFCs by late 1998 and early 1999. At the same time, the IPv4 standards are still standards and are likely to remain standards as long as IPv4 is widely implemented and deployed. When two versions of the same protocol coexist, it is necessary to document how the two versions are related.

What happens when a revised protocol replaces the older version? The revised protocol must go through the same process, and the older version may be retired unless a sufficiently large installed base uses the older version. Consider the Post Office Protocol (POP): POP version 2, documented in RFC 937, was designated historical after POP version 3 became STD-53 (RFC 1939).

Sometimes a standard becomes obsolete because a new protocol does the job much better. The Exterior Gateway Protocol (EGP), documented in RFC 904, was once STD-18. However, other routing protocols have come to replace EGP as a core protocol for the Internet, and it has since been relegated to the status of historic protocol.

Resolving Problems

One of the stated goals of the Internet standards process is to be fair, and that requires mechanisms for resolving disputes over how the process is conducted. RFC 2026 sets out guidelines for resolving problems that occur within working groups as well as problems relating to the entire standards process. These are largely common sense, at least in an organizational framework.

Although two types of disagreements are considered for working group disputes, only a single set of guidelines is provided. The types of disagreements are divided between those where an individual believes that his or her views were not given adequate consideration by the working group and those where the individual believes that the working group made an incorrect choice that could result in harm to the group's results. The resolution process relies on discussing the problem first with the working group chair or chairs, who may involve others in the group as necessary. If the problem can not be resolved at that level, it can be escalated to the area director responsible for that working group; further escalation progresses to the full IESG, and finally to the court of last resort, the IAB.

If an individual disagrees with an action taken by the IESG, the process is similar, but starts with the IESG chair. From there, the problem may be escalated to the entire IESG and then to the IAB. The IAB can not change the IESG's decision, but suggests alternatives or directs that the IESG's decision be annulled and consideration of the matter started over.

In the event that the disagreement pertains to whether the procedure itself is sufficient and fair, as described in RFC 2026, an individual can petition the board of the Internet Society.

Documenting the Process

All the groups involved in doing standards work are expected to make public their activities. This means that IETF and working group meetings must be announced on the IETF-announce mailing list. It also means that the IETF, the IESG, the IAB, all IETF working groups, and the Internet Society board must all make public their charters, minutes of their standards-related meetings, archives of working group mailing lists, and anything contributed in writing from participants in the standards process. Even expired I-Ds are archived by the IETF secretariat so as to maintain an historical record of standards activities.

IETF Workgroups

IETF working groups are designed to foster cooperation among individuals who work in widely disparate environments, from academic researchers to for-profit product developers. Working groups are also likely to include individuals who work for organizations with conflicting goals, incorporating people who work for competing software, hardware, and service vendors. Further complicating matters, working group members may live and work almost anywhere in the world.

Despite these difficulties, the bulk of the work of the IETF is accomplished by its working groups. RFC 2418 is appropriately titled "IETF Working Group Guidelines and Procedures." Describing how the working groups fit into the standards process while also outlining how successful working groups achieve their goals, this RFC should be required reading not only for anyone interested in the Internet standards process but also for anyone interested in organizational dynamics.

Defining the Working Group

An IETF working group is usually formed for the purpose of solving some specific problem or to create some specific result or results. For example, the Calendaring and Scheduling working group is chartered to "create standards that make calendaring and scheduling software significantly more useful and to enable a new class of solutions to be built that are only viable if open standards exist" (from the Calendaring and Scheduling working group charter, at www.ietf.org/html .charters/calsch-charter.html). The charter goes on to define three specific sets of problems relating to Internet calendaring and scheduling applications.

Working group deliverables are usually in the form of specifications, guidelines, or other reports published as RFCs. Once all tasks are completed, the working group may be disbanded or its operations may be suspended, with periodic review of standards as they progress through the standards track.

In keeping with the IETF's openness, IETF working groups are open to participation by anyone who wishes to contribute. Although much of the working groups' work is accomplished by small central cores of group members, other members can contribute through participation in working group mailing lists or by attending meetings in person. Again, inclusiveness reigns: Any activity that occurs at a physical meeting is reported to the mailing list, and rough consensus of the entire group is always a requirement. The working group chair can restrict contributions from members deemed to be acting counter to the interest of the group. If someone holds up meetings by discussing matters that are not appropriate or raising issues that are counter to the rough consensus, that person may be restricted from speaking, but not from attending the meeting.

There must be at least one working group chair, but usually no more than two. The chair's concern is to make "forward progress through a fair and open process" (from RFC 2418). It is up to the chair to ensure that the working group is accomplishing the tasks it is chartered to complete and nothing more or less. Other working group chair tasks include moderating the working group email list, planning working group sessions, communicating the results of the sessions, managing the work by motivating participants to do what needs to be done, developing and publishing supporting documents, and keeping track of implementations based on the working group's activities. Of course, this is a lot of work, and the chair may delegate some or all of these tasks.

Other working group staff include the secretary, who is responsible for taking minutes and recording working group decisions, and the document editor, who is responsible for ensuring that the documents the group generates truly reflect the decisions that have been made by the group. A working group facilitator, responsible for making sure that the group processes are working, may also be part of the group. The facilitator works on the style of interaction among the group members, rather than the content, to keep the group moving toward its goals. Finally, in certain cases, the IETF Area Director may assign a working group consultant to a working group. The consultant's role is to provide the benefit of his or her experience and technical expertise to the working group.

Working group members are likely to be called upon to serve on a design team. When a problem needs solving, the group may determine that a subset of the group should form a design team to solve it. Design teams can be completely informal, consisting of whoever happens to be standing around during a hallway chat, or they may be formally designated groups appointed by the working group chair to address some controversial issue, or something in between.

Working group guidelines are truly guidelines, and the working group chair is accorded considerable latitude in terms of how the working group's goals are to be achieved. As long as the process is fair and open and meets the basic requirements set forth in RFC 2418, the working group controls its own process.

A working group can be created only when certain conditions are met, and those conditions help define what working groups actually are able to do. The next section explains this process.

Creating a Working Group

Working groups are created at the behest of an IETF Area Director or by some other individual or group. The Area Director has to get behind the idea for the new group, although the IESG (with advice from the IAB) has the final say over whether the group is formed. The Area Director considers the following criteria before making any decision about pushing forward with the chartering process. These criteria help define what a working group should be, inasmuch as any existing working group should meet most if not all of them:

Clarity and relevance to the Internet community. Is there a clear vision of what the working group should be working on, and will the working group be working on something that is of value to the Internet community? Without clear goals and relevance, a proposed working group is unlikely to be chartered.

Specific and achievable goals. The working group should have specific goals that can be attained within a reasonable period of time. Working groups are meant to have finite lifetimes, and they are meant to actually perform complete tasks.

Risks and urgency. What happens if the working group is not formed? What risks are incurred if no action is taken, and what risks might be incurred if action *is* taken? Working groups that target problems that hinder Internet scalability and continued growth may get priority treatment.

Overlap with existing working groups. Will the proposed working group's activities duplicate efforts being made by any existing working groups? Will the proposed working group be working on the same or similar problems being addressed by any existing working groups? Overlap may not be bad if the new working group approaches the problem from a different technical direction. However, if only a limited number of qualified people are working on the problem, multiple working groups could cause those people's efforts to be spread a bit thin.

Interest level. Enough people must be interested in doing the work of the working group, as well as in participating as working group staff (that is, working group chair, secretary, and so on). According to RFC 2418, a viable working group requires that at least four or five people be interested in the management of the group and at least one to two dozen others must be willing to participate to the extent of attending meetings and contributing to the mailing list. The RFC also notes that the group membership must be broadly based. It is not sufficient for membership to represent a single organization, which would be viewed as an attempt by that organization to create its own Internet standard.

Expertise level. Are there enough people within the IETF who are sufficiently knowledgeable about the working group work to make worthwhile contributions, and are enough of those people interested in participating? Again, the objective of the working group is to accomplish specific objectives. If the working group members aren't experienced in the technologies they are working with, it's unlikely they'll be able to achieve those goals.

End-user interest level. Is there a consumer base for the output of the working group? Are end users interested in seeing the goals proposed by the working group charter accomplished? The IETF is an engineering organization, whose production is intended for use by end users. Pure-research projects are better accomplished by the IRTF; the IETF must concern itself with products that have practical applications.

Practicality of IETF involvement. All the criteria listed here might be met, but some specifications are better produced by other bodies. There may be interest, expertise, relevance, and all the rest, but the IETF is unlikely to get involved with developing standards for LAN media or object models. Other bodies are better qualified to produce specifications in these areas.

Intellectual property rights issues. Increasingly, intellectual property rights—software patents, copyrights, and more—are relevant to work being done by working groups. These issues must be understood before the working group is chartered.

Open technology. Many organizations would like to have their proprietary standards recognized as Internet standards. Such recognition would accord the organization a significant advantage over competitors. When evaluating applications for new working groups, the IESG must attempt to determine whether the work planned by the group is an attempt to favor some existing, closed technology, or whether the plan is devised to solicit IETF participation to genuinely develop an open specification.

Understanding of the technologies and issues. Are the issues and technologies proposed for the working group's activities well understood? Technologies should be reasonably mature before they are brought into an Internet standards effort. The IESG would prefer to avoid the kind of debacle that could result from rushing into unproven technology.

Overlap with other standards bodies. Do the working group's goals intersect with the goals of any other standards bodies? This may not be cause for concern if the working group approaches the issues in a way unique for the Internet, but the IESG would have to evaluate the degree to which liaison with the other group exists or is required.

Once the Area Director is satisfied that a working group proposal is in good shape, the chartering process starts. The Area Director and the person who is to become the working group chair work out the charter together and then submit it to the IESG for approval and to the IAB for review. The charter includes a description of the working group and its objectives and goals, scheduled milestones necessary to achieve those goals, and a list of administrative details like names and contact information for working group chair(s).

Working Group Operations

Working groups have a certain amount of latitude in how they operate, as long as the procedures that result are open and fair. Most of the action usually takes place on the mailing list, with members of the group suggesting options, debating the value of different approaches, and discussing problems arising from implementation and deployment of the solutions being considered by the working group.

The standard for moving working group tasks forward is rough consensus, meaning that most of the group is mostly agreed about the solution in question. Determining where the rough consensus actually is, is the job of the working group chair. This can be difficult when all work is carried on over the mailing list, but it is certainly possible. Consensus can also be determined at meetings, where the group can vote in some way. In either case, when the chair feels that a consensus has been reached, the chair may solicit comments from the list or call for a vote. No hard and fast rule determines where consensus actually lies in terms of how many are in favor and how many opposed: The only guideline provided in RFC 2418 is that agreement by 51 percent of the group is not enough to form a rough consensus, and when the group is 99 percent in agreement, a more than rough consensus definitely does exist.

Working Group Documentation

First and foremost, the raw activity of the working group is available in the archives for the working group mailing list. Here you will find all the comments, arguments, proposals, and questions raised in the group. You will also find agendas for physical meetings, meeting minutes, and notifications about the publication of other working group documents, particularly Internet-Drafts and RFCs. Anyone interested in the output of a particular IETF working group should subscribe to the mailing list right away.

For a more formal look at the results of the work of a working group, look at the Internet-Drafts it generates. Although these are definitely working documents, they do reflect the best and most recent version of the working group's product. An I-D may be revised many times before it is finally approved and published as an RFC, but only one version of the I-D is ever publicly available at any given time. To trace the development of a specification across time, you must either follow the mailing list or download and store copies of each new revision of the I-D. However, most I-D revisions include a section detailing the changes made since the previous version.

The ultimate documentation of a working group's activity is the finished RFCs it generates. An I-D is just a draft, and six months after it is published, it expires unless it can be moved forward. RFCs, on the other hand, live forever and contain information that is at least of some interest to the Internet community and that may actually describe a specification on the Internet standards track.

Reading List

Table 4.1 lists some RFCs that elaborate on the information presented in this chapter.

Table 4.1   Relevant RFCs

RFC	TITLE	DESCRIPTION
RFC 2026	The Internet Standards Process—Revision 3	This document serves as the basis of much of this chapter and explains the exact process by which specifications become standards.
RFC 2418	IETF Working Group Guidelines and Procedures	This document explains how working groups work, how to start one, how to run one, and how to terminate one.
RFC 2028	Organizations Involved in the IETF Standards Process	This RFC explains what organizational entities are involved in the process of setting standards, as well as what roles each plays.

Table 4.1   *(Continued)*

RFC	TITLE	DESCRIPTION
RFC 1796	Not All RFCs Are Standards	This short RFC simply punctuates the distinction between acceptance of a specification as a standard and acceptance of a specification for publication as an RFC.
RFC 2223	Instructions to RFC Authors	This RFC is useful for anyone wishing to write an RFC or RFC-like document as well as for those interested in how these documents are styled and structured.

Getting the RFCs

You can find RFCs in lots of places, though some are more complete, accurate, and up-to-date than others. In this chapter, we examine where to find RFCs and Internet-Drafts, and where to get the latest information about RFCs and Internet-Drafts.

RFCs can be found almost everywhere, it seems. Computer book authors have been known to include complete copies of RFCs in their books, and some authors incorporate searchable databases of RFCs on CD-ROMs included with their books. Yahoo! may have as many as a dozen or so RFC-related sites, most of which are archives containing all (or almost all) RFCs published to date. I've included a handful of the Web archive sites I find most useful, and you can find more pointers on the companion Web site for this book. However, anyone interested in getting the latest should do his or her own search for RFC-related Web sites: Old ones go away, new ones come online all the time, and the ones that stay on often undergo changes, sometimes for the better and sometimes for the worse.

Having all the RFCs does not necessarily give you everything you need to work with RFCs, however. For one thing, there are somewhere in the neighborhood of 2,500 different RFCs. Trying to find what you need in that thicket of documents is sort of like trying to find what you need in an encyclopedia whose articles are arranged in the order they were written. To make things worse, revisions of existing articles are simply treated as newer articles, and the older, outdated articles are never removed. And, of course, there is no index.

To make sense of RFCs, you need something to act as an index. In most cases, that something is a search tool associated with the Web site or CD-ROM where the RFCs themselves are published. RFC archives may be totally spartan, like the directory published by the IETF, which is nothing more than an FTP directory containing the RFC files. More elaborate archives provide tools for searching and displaying the RFCs, with varying degrees of success. So far, no single site provides everything you need to work with RFCs, but some combination of two or three should be sufficient to meet most needs.

Staying on Top of RFCs

There are several different types of RFC consumers. The more casual consumers are usually more interested in looking up some specific standard or document on a one-time or infrequent basis. A network manager may consult an RFC to check on header fields or some other aspect of a protocol while troubleshooting a network problem. Computer science students may consult the RFC archives to document some protocol. Students of history may consult the RFC archives to track down some Internet-related event. The casual reader may have been given an RFC number by a text reference (like this one), a vendor, a professor, or some other source, and thus may have no need for any type of search engine. Casual RFC readers often find out about new Internet standards-track specification from their vendors or from trade press reports about new products that support them.

People involved with deploying Internet-based or related systems may have a higher level of interest in RFCs. Intranet/extranet managers need to understand what their systems are doing and how they do it. This includes understanding the protocols as well as how vendors implement those protocols. These users need to be able to search for RFCs based on keywords. They need to be able to jump from one RFC to another related RFC to see how they affect each other. They need to know which RFC is a current standard (or nonstandard) and which is obsolete or experimental.

These readers may even need to know when a new specification has been added to the standards track or when an existing specification advances along the standards track.

The third class of RFC readers are those who not only need access to current RFCs, but who must know what future RFCs will look like. These are the implementers—network software and hardware engineers who must translate the specifications from document form into products that actually do something. Not only must these implementers know when new specifications are published as RFCs or advanced along the standards track, but they must have a pretty good idea of where the specification is going well before it is published as an RFC. Vendors implement specifications described in Internet-Drafts for experimentation and testing so they can roll out RFC-compliant products quickly once the RFC is published.

This book was written for people in the two latter categories, and in the next section we look at some of the more important mailing lists to which you should subscribe if you need timely information about RFCs.

IETF Mailing Lists

Several mailing lists are worth knowing about if you are interested in what the IETF is doing:

IETF-discuss. The IETF discussions list is an open forum for IETF members to discuss issues related to the Internet, the IETF, the IESG, and their activities. If you are considering subscribing to this list, check out the archives at the IETF Web site.

IETF-announce. The IETF announcement list is used to distribute information about the logistics of IETF meetings, agendas for IETF meetings, actions taken on working group activities, announcements of Internet-Drafts, IESG last calls, Internet standard actions, and announcements of publication of new RFCs. This is a read-only list, and it is used to communicate official activities of the IETF and IESG, rather than to stimulate discussion.

Internet Monthly Report. Subscribers to this mailing list receive copies of a monthly report detailing all the activities of participating organizations during the month preceding. In this report, you can find a summary of all standard actions, new RFCs and Internet-Drafts published, activities of the RFC editor and the IANA, information about meetings that were held during the month, and notices of relevant meetings to come.

RFC-dist. This is the RFC distribution list. Subscribers receive notification every time a new RFC is published, along with a URL pointing to the newly published document.

To avoid duplication of messages, most people would choose to subscribe to only one of the IETF-announce, RFC-dist, or Internet Monthly Report lists. For example, if you want notification every time a new RFC is published but are not interested in Internet-Drafts or any other Internet actions, you would subscribe to the RFC-dist list. If you don't want to be bombarded with messages but still want to stay on top of Internet standards activities, you would subscribe to the Internet Monthly Report. If you need to know everything that happens, as it happens, you would subscribe to the IETF-announce list. All RFC-dist list messages are copied to the IETF-announce list, as is the Internet Monthly Report, so subscribing to the IETF-announce list is the most comprehensive option.

Table 5.1 includes subscription information for these lists as well URLs for list archives. Before subscribing, readers are urged to visit the archive sites listed in Table 5.1 and read all instructions about the mailing list before subscribing.

Table 5.1 Addresses for Subscribing to IETF-related Mailing Lists

MAILING LIST	EMAIL ADDRESS	ARCHIVE SITE	NOTES
RFC-dist	majordomo@ zephyr.isi.edu	(included in IETF announce list archive)	Message body should read "subscribe rfc-dist".
IETF-announce	ietf-announce-request@ietf.org	www.ietf.org/mail-archive/ietf-announce/maillist.html	Use "subscribe" as both the subject line and the message body.
Internet Monthly Report	majordomo@ isi.edu	ftp://ftp.isi.edu/in-notes/imr/	Message body should read "subscribe imr".
IETF Discussion List	ietf-request@ ietf.org	www.ietf.org/mail-archive/ietf/maillist.html	Use "subscribe" as both the subject line and the message body.

NOTE The IETF discussion list can be very noisy at times—it is an open forum from which no one may be ejected and without any type of censorship. Participants sometimes veer off onto topics not relevant to the IETF, post repetitively on the same topic, or return to topics that are no longer relevant or that have already been discussed into the ground. An alternative exists for people who are busy and want to know what's being discussed, without the cross-postings, postings from known troublemakers, and repeated requests for help in unsubscribing. The *ietf+censored* list filters out much of the noise and can be subscribed to by sending a message to *ietf+censored-request@alvestrand.no* with the body *"subscribe."*

For those interested in seeing only the rejected messages (for amusement purposes only), send a message body of *subscribe* to the address *ietf+censored-rejects-request@alvestrand.no.*

For more information about these lists, see *www.alvestrand.no/ietf+censored.html.*

RFC Archives

Dozens of RFC archives scattered over the globe exist on the Internet. Some are more useful than others, and some are better than others. The RFC archive on the IETF site contains the raw RFCs as text files and, in some cases, as PostScript files. However, this is simply a file transfer site: There are no search tools here. If you need help with RFCs, you need to find another resource.

Rather than list all the RFC archives currently available, this section discusses how to locate archives and what kinds of features are available in RFC archives. Links to some of the better RFC archives are available on the companion Web site to this book; readers are urged to make their own search for a source that is appropriate for them.

Finding RFC Archives

Locating an RFC archive on the Internet is relatively simple. Try the RFC editor Web site for a list of some RFC archives:

www.rfc-editor.org/rfc.html

This is a good place to start because it describes some of the features and capabilities of the listed sites.

Portal sites like Yahoo! also maintain categories related to Internet standards. Yahoo! even has a category just for RFCs (http://dir.yahoo .com/Computers_and_Internet/Standards/RFCs/), which is a fertile hunting ground for RFC archive sites. Portals may offer more selection, including off-beat archive sites.

If you don't find what you want at a portal site, you can try one of the Web search sites like AltaVista, HotBot, or others. A search on the word "RFC" will undoubtedly produce thousands of matches, but you can narrow it down by adding qualifying words such as "archive," "search," or "standards." You may also be able to narrow the search down to geographic areas or languages: HotBot offers criteria based on domain, continent, and language as well as the more common Boolean searches on words.

RFC Archive Features

RFC archives usually offer a mix of features, and some mixtures are more useful than others. Some archives are simply that: repositories for raw RFC files. If you know the RFC number, you can use these archives; if not, you may be out of luck. Some of these file dumps actually list the RFC names, authors, and date of publication in addition to the number, so you can use your browser's search function to find relevant documents as long as you know what to look for.

At a minimum, the archive should provide a search function. Searching should be done on the body of the RFC text, rather than just on RFC titles. Some archives' searches are too restrictive and produce way too few hits; other archives' searches are too loose and produce way too many hits. The "just right" number of hits varies from person to person, but the search results should include all the relevant RFCs without including too many irrelevant ones.

Consider too the search features. Some archives permit only simple searches on one or more terms; others permit Boolean text searches. Some archives allow you to fine-tune your searches, limiting the number of hits; others restrict you to a maximum number of hits and urge you to add terms if you exceed that maximum. Some allow complex searches with criteria relating to the title and body of the RFCs, as well as options regarding the output of the results. The more control you have over the search, the more likely you are to find just the documents you want.

Some archive sites include only RFCs, while others provide access to Internet-Drafts as well. Likewise, some archive sites allow you to search or browse through document subsets, such as the STD, BCP, and FYI series of RFCs.

Finally, some sites even include hyperlinking: RFCs (and possibly other documents) cited in the body of the RFC you are reading are activated at Web links. Open up one RFC, and you can immediately jump to any RFC cited in the text by clicking on it. This is a great idea, but the implementations tend to fall short. The RFC being displayed usually links to itself through the RFC number listed in the page headers. One version actually seems to link any number with three or more digits, including zip codes and binary values of fields included in protocol descriptions.

RFCs by Email

For those with email-only access to the Internet, RFCs are available by email from the RFC-INFO service. Send email to rfc-info@isi.edu and format your message body like this:

Retrieve: RFC

Doc-ID: RFC####

Replace #### with the number of the RFC you want, padding the value with zeros for RFC numbers that are lower than 1000. For example, to retrieve RFC 821, you would use *RFC0821*.

For additional features or for help with retrieving RFCs by email, you can send a message to rfc-info@isi.edu with the message body *help: help*.

Getting Internet-Drafts

Subscribing to the IETF-announce mailing list will get you, among other things, announcements of publication of all new I-Ds. These announcements include URLs you can use to retrieve a copy of the I-D. You may also want to search for I-Ds that relate to a particular technology or issue.

You can see all I-Ds generated by a particular IETF working group at the active working group Web page:

www.ietf.org/html.charters/wg-dir.html

Choose the working group of interest from this list, and you'll see all its RFCs and I-Ds. Many related organizations also maintain archives of I-Ds as well as RFCs; for example, the Internet Mail Consortium maintains RFCs and I-Ds related to Internet mail at its Web site:

www.imc.org/mail-standards.html

The IETF maintains the most up-to-date and comprehensive list of I-Ds. The main repository for Internet-Drafts is at:

www.ietf.org/ID.html

From this page, you can do a keyword search, browse through the I-D directory, or view guidelines for I-D authors. Many of the other good RFC repositories also include facilities for searching for I-Ds.

Reading List

Rather than suggest any specific references for additional reading in this chapter, you should go to your favorite Web search or portal site to search for RFC archives. If you can't find at least five, try another search engine. Now, try each of the archive sites you've located and see which one best suits you.

Regardless of whether you do your own search, be sure to visit Lynn Wheeler's IETF RFC Index site (www.garlic.com/~lynn/rfcietf.html). It is one of the most comprehensive and useful archives around. Wheeler provides the ability to view specifications at different stages of the standards track as well as view-only specific document series. Also included here are links to specifications that have been made obsolete as well as the specifications that have replaced them. Links to related sites are also useful.

Reading the RFCs

As mentioned in Chapter 5, "Getting the RFCs," RFC consumers tend to fall into three categories: casual readers, deployers, and developers. Just as each type of consumer has slightly different requirements for obtaining and tracking RFCs and Internet-Drafts, so too does each type of consumer use these documents in a different way. This chapter takes a look at how people use RFCs.

Though it may not be apparent from reading some of the earlier RFCs, new Internet documents must conform to a very specific set of stylistic requirements. RFC 2223, "Instructions to RFC Authors," is a must-read for anyone who plans to write an Internet-Draft or RFC. It is also useful for understanding just what is and is not included in an RFC.

All RFCs are published as ASCII text files because it is a universal format, accessible to anyone with email or better Internet access. Occasionally an RFC may also be published in PostScript to provide additional detail to graphics included in the document, but most ASCII RFCs include text-based graphics. All modern RFCs adhere to a strict page format, with headers that contain the RFC number, title, and month and year of publication and footers that contain the author(s), RFC category (informational, standards-track, best current practices, or experimental), and page number. The first page displays the RFC number, the authors' names, their organizational affiliation, and a line indicating which previous RFCs the current one updates or makes obsolete. If the document has any other numbers, for example an STD, FYI, or BCP number, these are listed at the top of the first page as well.

RFCs must have a status section, identifying the RFC as documenting a standards track specification, a best current practice (BCP), an experimental specification, or an informational document. The status section consists of one of four boilerplate paragraphs, each one indicating a different type of document. A brief boilerplate copyright notice, reserving copyright for the Internet Society, is also required on the first page, with a longer piece of boilerplate added at the end of the document.

The introduction section briefly describes the document itself. This section is often the most useful when the reader is searching for a particular specification. The introduction summarizes the RFC, usually in a few paragraphs or less. The introduction section is usually derived from the abstract section of its precursor Internet-Draft.

Other required sections for RFCs include a references section citing all previously published documents to which the RFC refers and a security considerations section discussing potential security issues raised by the RFC. The author's address section is also required, as it permits readers to send questions or comments directly to the author.

Of course, these sections are the shell within which the meat of the RFC is nestled. After the introduction, the specification is described in detail. The first section after the introduction often describes pertinent terminology and may be followed by a section or sections describing the requirements or circumstances that caused the specification to be written. The protocol headers and fields are then described, followed by discussion of specific protocol features and how they work. The last sections may discuss how the protocol interacts with other protocols, how it should be implemented or deployed, or any other issues that need to be addressed in order to implement the protocol. Appendices are often used where appropriate.

RFCs usually describe behaviors and attributes of protocols. They tell you how a system using the protocol should work. From there, you can build your own implementation of the protocol. RFCs don't usually explain how to build the implementations, they just tell you how an implementation would work if it were built. Some RFCs describe protocol

APIs, but these still describe how the implementations must behave rather than how to actually program the implementations.

Understanding Protocols

Perhaps the most common use of RFCs is to understand what the protocol being specified actually does and how it works. Casual readers as well as developers must first look to the RFC for a basic understanding before anything else can happen. Casual readers may be able to stop there, although both deployers and developers need to look beyond a basic understanding of the specification to meet their needs.

Getting a basic understanding of a protocol may be as simple as reading the introduction section of the RFC; this is often all that is necessary. However, things are not always that simple. Sometimes it is necessary to read through the entire RFC, and even then the answer may not be apparent. In those cases, it may be worthwhile to check on the citations in the RFC reference section as well as any related or dependent specifications. When all else fails, the casual reader may need to take a short course in TCP/IP internetworking.

Reading the RFCs

Always start with the introduction. This usually is the most precise and concise summary of the specification available anywhere. The introduction usually explains what the protocol does and how it does it. You can often rule out an RFC as being irrelevant by looking at the introduction. You may also determine that a protocol does what you want it to do, the way you want to do it, by reading the introduction.

More often, you will need to delve further into the RFC to find what you need. Sometimes you will have to pay careful attention to the definitions section, especially if the specification refers to systems or processes with which you are unfamiliar. Sometimes the definitions will be mostly formalized descriptions of terms that are well understood. Read any sections that discuss the background of the problem that the specification solves or attempts to solve. This section may describe not only the approach used by the specification described in the RFC but also other competitive or precursor solutions.

Most casual readers will have found their answer by now. Most of the basics of the protocol and its special features are outlined in the first few sections of the RFC; reading beyond that into the protocol nitty-gritty of headers and detailed specifications may not provide answers to simple questions. At this point, it may be useful to look at references and protocol dependencies rather than attempting to divine further meaning from the RFC in question.

Checking References and Dependencies

If the reader simply wants to understand the broad outlines of the protocol, sometimes more background is needed rather than more detail about the specification being examined. Internet protocol specifications often expand as they are updated, especially as they progress along the standards track. A specification that is sufficient for a proposed standard usually expands over time as people uncover potential problems or issues related to the deployment of the protocol on the Internet. RFCs of updated protocols tend to expand in order to deal with, or at least acknowledge, these issues and problems.

To understand the basic concepts of a revised specification, it is sometimes useful to go back to the original specification. Likewise, documents cited in the references section often include discussions of the issues and approaches and concepts used as background for development of the specification described in the RFC. Often, the documents are other RFCs or Internet-Drafts and are easily accessible online.

An RFC can specify a new version, update, or replacement for an existing specification. For example, when a proposed standard has been revised and moved to draft standard status, the new version is given a new RFC number. However, just looking at the original, proposed standard RFC will not give you any indication that the RFC has been deprecated. Relations between RFCs are indicated in Lynn Wheeler's RFC Web site (www.garlic.com/~lynn/rfcietf.html).

Getting More Help

When reading the RFC doesn't help and the references are similarly unenlightening, the casual reader may need more internetworking background. Books like *TCP/IP Clearly Explained, 3rd edition* (Pete Loshin, Morgan Kaufman 1999) or *Illustrated TCP/IP* (Matthew Naugle, Wiley 1998) provide general readers with enough background to begin to read RFCs with greater understanding of the basic concepts of internetworking.

Alternatively, casual readers can often find answers to technical questions, or at least pointers to good sources for such answers, on mailing lists and newsgroups devoted to the protocol specified in the RFC. Public newsgroups are available for most Internet protocols, as are FAQs for those groups. Mailing lists maintained by the relevant IETF working group are often helpful, though the reader is still urged to check the list archives or read a few days' worth of newsgroup postings to see what kinds of questions are encouraged and to see whether the question has recently been answered.

RFC Troubleshooting

From "what does this protocol do?" to "why doesn't this protocol work?" is a big step. Deployers of protocols need to be able to read the specifications with a more critical eye than most casual readers. They need to understand not only how to identify which protocol is at fault and how protocols behave, but also how to look at network traffic and determine what is actually going on.

Casual readers often know exactly what protocol and even what RFC they should be looking for: They may have been told that a certain specification solves their problems or is incorporated into a new networking product they are considering for purchase. Troubleshooters have no such assurances. More often, the people involved with troubleshooting products that have been deployed know only that some system is not working as they believe it should be working. They must first analyze the problem and rule out the more commonplace causes before they need to examine the protocol specifications.

Protocol analysis tools capture and decode network traffic. Network managers can examine protocol behaviors by looking at the traffic being sent and received by local systems. Initial descriptions of network problems usually are phrased in terms of lack of connectivity between systems or failure of system functions despite apparent connectivity. The solution usually lies in something external to the protocol, or at least in some issue relating to the installation or configuration of the protocol implementation.

Network support staff are usually able to solve problems through the process of elimination: Misconfigured systems, disabled servers, or overly strict firewalls account for a large portion of these problems. Network engineers using protocol analyzers can eliminate the peskier problems that relate to protocol implementations by studying the actual network transmissions and determining whether the implementations are behaving as they are supposed to.

Problems with implementations can also be tracked down by replacing the problem system or systems with other systems known to work correctly. Scanning network transmissions, the engineers can determine whether the functionally equivalent systems are actually behaving in the same ways. Even though Internet standards are well defined, as are the requirements for implementing them, not all implementations are created equal. An implementation may be incomplete or incorrect either through design or in error, but to detect a problem you must understand what the implementation is supposed to do, as defined in the relevant RFC.

Deployment professionals who are reading RFCs for troubleshooting purposes must be able to go beyond the basics of the specification and understand the specific functions defined by the protocol. Thus, it is not enough to understand that TCP, for example, uses four different timing functions to guarantee service across a virtual circuit. You must also understand exactly how those timers are supposed to work and why performance can be disrupted if one or more of them is improperly implemented.

Newsgroups and mailing lists are far more important tools for the deployment professional than the casual RFC reader, as they are sources of information about specific implementations as well as good places to ask technical questions. Whereas basic questions about a protocol are less welcome in such forums, issues about how protocol implementations actually work are central to the operation of the IETF working groups as well as to participants on newsgroups and mailing lists.

Building Protocol Implementations

No one has a greater need to be on top of the Internet standards process than the people responsible for building the applications that implement standard protocols. Any implementer who waits for a specification to achieve full Internet standard status loses all hope of ever attaining significant market share without huge cost. This is what happened to Microsoft when it first started building Internet software. Microsoft started building its Web browser long after Netscape and Spyglass dominated the market. Ultimately, Microsoft garnered significant share only by giving away its browser and by bundling it into as many products and packages as it could manage. In effect, Microsoft had to start from scratch in order to catch up; in fact, Microsoft licensed browser code from Spyglass before building its own browser.

Having learned from experience, Microsoft now participates in many IETF working groups. Not only does Microsoft gain access to valuable information about what the new and revised standards will look like, but it also guides those efforts through the working groups.

If you want to implement a protocol for a commercial product or service, you are not alone. If you want your product to succeed, it must be timely, and that means, at the least, tracking protocol development from the Internet-Draft phase. Ideally, protocol implementers actively participate in the standards development process through working group mailing lists and by attending working group meetings.

Understanding the Standards

The relevant protocol is not always immediately apparent, nor is there only a single relevant protocol for a particular application. A developer working on collaborative workgroup software may be affected by specifications relating to Internet messaging, calendaring and scheduling, IP multicast, multimedia data transmission, and quality of service. Switch and router developers must stay abreast of all developments relating to IP routing as well as to data link layer transports like Ethernet, ATM, Frame Relay, FDDI, and others.

Understanding the standards means not just reading the relevant RFCs and Internet-Drafts, but also looking at existing implementations. The IETF maintains reports on implementations of Internet standards (at www.ietf.org/IESG/implementation.html). Prospective implementers are advised to start here by looking at existing implementations and reports about those implementations (there is some talk of enhancing the IETF's role in making reference implementations of standard protocols available).

It's important to remember that by working within the system, implementers have access to far more information and assistance than is incorporated into the RFCs.

Reading List

The best way to get comfortable with reading RFCs is by simply reading an RFC that covers a topic that is of interest. In addition to the RFCs listed in previous chapters, you can use your preferred mechanism to search for an RFC on some aspect of Ethernet, and then simply try to make sense of it.

As you read, try to answer some questions:

- What kind of RFC is it? (e.g., informational, standards track, etc.)

- Does the RFC belong to some other document series? (e.g., BCP, STD, FYI, etc.)

- Is there any way you can use the RFC to confirm that a behavior or characteristic of some familiar application or system complies with the RFC?

- Can you locate any of the RFC's references, to gain greater insight into the RFC you just read?

All of these exercises should help you master the art of reading RFCs.

Network Management Fundamentals

The Simple Network Management Protocol (SNMP) uses a very clever architecture for monitoring and managing network devices, services, functions, and performance. The SNMP architecture relies on what is, in effect, a vastly distributed database. Every monitored device stores information about itself in a rigorously structured format, conforming to a database schema called a Management Information Base (MIB). MIBs consist of objects and events that are defined using a Structure of Management Information (SMI). SNMP defines a set of rules for management applications to access the information stored in an MIB, as well as to modify that information when and where appropriate.

Different MIBs are defined for different types of systems. Any device connected to an IP network is required to maintain a certain minimum required set of information pertaining to IP nodes. A device acting as a server may be required to support a different set of MIB modules in addition to the basic MIB for IP nodes. Depending on the node's network interface, additional MIB modules may be desirable.

In this chapter, we review the standards behind the SNMP network management architecture: SNMP itself, SMI, and MIB. We also discuss the need for adding managed objects specific to a node's network interface. In Chapter 14, we introduce the specific Internet standard network management specifications relevant to managing nodes in an ATM network.

Internet Standard Management Framework

According to RFC 2570, "Introduction to Version 3 of the Internet-Standard Network Management Framework," any organization that uses the Internet Standard Management Framework contains these four basic components:

Managed nodes. RFC 2570 specifies the number as "several (typically many)." A managed node contains an SNMP agent that can provide information to network management entities.

One or more SNMP managers. In other words, at least one management application can solicit or collect information from the managed nodes.

A protocol for transferring management information among SNMP entities. In other words, this refers to the Simple Network Management Protocol.

Management information. This is the information that the SNMP agents make available to SNMP managers and that the managers can use to determine things such as how much traffic is going through a particular interface or what kind of machine is connected to a particular interface.

These are the actual things that get deployed in a managed network. The things themselves are specified in conformance with (what else) a set of Internet specifications and go beyond the protocol that defines how information gets passed from a managed node to a manager. The management framework has a modular architecture that, according to RFC 2570, includes the following:

- A data definition language
- A definition of the management information
- A definition of the protocol
- Security and administration

The SMI provides a language for management information, while the MIB uses the SMI to define management information. The SNMP specification defines the protocol, and a series of other specifications defines the rules for network management security and administration.

All these components are defined in RFCs. Table 7.1 shows some of the documents that describe this architecture, including which part of

Table 7.1 Components of the Internet Standard Management Framework

COMPONENT	RFC	STD	TITLE
Protocol definition	1157	15	Simple Network Management Protocol (SNMP)
Data definition language	1212		Concise MIB Definitions
Definition of management	1213		Management Information Base for Network Management of TCP/IP-information Based Internets: MIB-II
Protocol definition	1905		Protocol Operations for Version 2 of the Simple Network Management Protocol (SNMPv2)
Protocol definition	1906		Transport Mappings for Version 2 of the Simple Network Management Protocol (SNMPv2)
Definition of management information	1907		Management Information Base for Version 2 of the Simple Network Management Protocol (SNMPv2)
Protocol definition	2570		Introduction to Version 3 of the Internet-Standard Network Management Framework
Protocol definition	2571		An Architecture for Describing SNMP Management Frameworks
Protocol definition	2572		Message Processing and Dispatching for the Simple Network Management Protocol (SNMP)
Security and administration	2573		SNMP Applications
Security and administration	2574		The User-Based Security Model for Version 3 of the Simple Network Management Protocol (SNMPv3)
Security and administration	2575		View-Based Access Control Model for the Simple Network Management Protocol (SNMP)
Data definition language	2578	58	Structure of Management Information Version 2 (SMIv2)
Data definition language	2579	58	Textual Conventions for SMIv2
Data definition language	2580	58	Conformance Statements for SMIv2

the architecture each RFC documents. Table 7.2 shows the many different MIB modules, which number close to 100, with more Internet-Draft MIB modules being submitted regularly.

The rest of this chapter outlines the basics of the SMI, followed by a discussion of how that structure is used to create the MIB. From there, we summarize how SNMP works, followed by a discussion of the Interfaces Group MIB and how it all relates to Ethernet.

Structure of Management Information

RFC 2578, "Structure of Management Information Version 2 (SMIv2)" (Internet standard STD-58), defines the schema to be used for the database that is the Management Information Base (MIB). Using the Abstract Syntax Notation One (ASN.1), RFC 2578 defines a framework for the data to be used by network management tools through SNMP.

Although a thorough discussion of ASN.1 and database schemas is beyond the scope of this text, a figure and an example help clarify matters. The SMI defines how any particular piece of information can be expressed and identified within the structure. Every piece of information or object is identified with an object identifier value, which is a unique value that authoritatively names an object. Each part of the object identifier describes, in successively greater precision, what object that object identifier refers to.

The object identifier is hierarchical, so that the leftmost value in the ID is the most general. When it has a value of 0, it indicates an object administered by the CCITT (now known as the ITU, but still referred to as the CCITT in this schema). When the value is 1, it indicates an object administered by the ISO. The value 2 indicates a jointly administered object. All things Internet are ISO objects (as are many other things, by the way), so the first part of their object ID is always 1.

Under the ISO are four subordinates, numbered 0 through 3. We're interested in the identified organizations subordinate, 3, because that's where the Defense Advanced Research Projects Agency (DARPA) can be found as a sub-subordinate (number 6). The Internet is number 1 under that subordinate. Thus, any Internet-related objects in this schema begin with the values:

```
1.3.6.1...
```

It doesn't stop there—for our purposes, that's very close to the beginning. As Figure 7.1 shows, the hierarchy continues down from there with several additional branches under Internet(1). As you can see, any object residing under the mib-2(1) object would be represented as:

```
1.3.6.1.2.1....
```

This structure makes it possible for one network entity (perhaps a network management application) to query another network entity (perhaps a managed server, client workstation, or even a printer) for information stored within this structure. All managed devices have this structure built in, and thus network management applications can simply request a value for a particular node by specifying the object identifier.

There is much more to SMI, of course. For one thing, there is the Abstract Syntax Notation One (ASN.1), an ISO standard for representing data. For another, there is considerable documentation of how ASN.1 is to be used and how to format and represent data within the SMI. However, this is beyond the scope of this book.

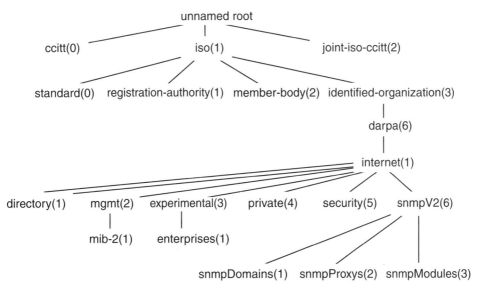

Figure 7.1   Structure of management information.

Management Information Base (MIB)

The SMI creates a framework within which to build a database. The MIB creates the actual database. Allowing each vendor to create its own management and administration database schema for each product would result in confusion: One vendor might call the field containing the number of packets processed by a router "PACKETS," while another might call it "PKTS_PROC." Instead, all vendors use the dot-delimited object representations to hold relevant data.

Originally intended to be a monolithic structure, defined by a single group, the MIB is clearly too big a task for any single entity to get its arms around. No single entity could be expected to know just what kind of information would be needed by an Ethernet hub as well as what would be needed by an ATM switch as well as what would be needed by all the other devices and servers for which MIBs have been defined. Table 7.2 shows a list of most of the RFCs defining MIBs, along with their status and standard number (where relevant). There are a lot, as you can see.

Table 7.2   MIB Documents

STATUS	NAME	RFC	STD
Standard	Concise MIB Definitions	1212	16
Standard	Management Information Base-II	1213	17
Experimental	CLNS-MIB	1238	
Proposed	Border Gateway Protocol MIB (Version 3)	1269	
Proposed	FDDI-MIB	1285	
Proposed	SNMP MIB Extension for X.25 LAPB	1381	
Proposed	SNMP MIB Extension for X.25 Packet Layer	1382	
Proposed	DS1/E1 Interface Type	1406	
Proposed	DS3/E3 Interface Type	1407	
Proposed	Identification MIB	1414	
Proposed	Multiprotocol Interconnect on X.25 MIB	1461	
Proposed	Link Control Protocol of PPP MIB	1471	
Proposed	Security Protocols of PPP MIB	1472	
Proposed	IP Network Control Protocol of PPP MIB	1473	

Table 7.2 *(Continued)*

STATUS	NAME	RFC	STD
Proposed	Bridge PPP MIB	1474	
Draft	BRIDGE-MIB	1493	
Proposed	FDDI Management Information Base	1512	
Proposed	Token Ring Extensions to RMON MIB	1513	
Proposed	Host Resources MIB	1514	
Proposed	802.3 MAU MIB	1515	
Proposed	Source Routing Bridge MIB	1525	
Draft	DECNET MIB	1559	
Proposed	X.500 Directory Monitoring MIB	1567	
Proposed	Evolution of the Interfaces Group of MIB-II Elective	1573	
Proposed	MIB SONET/SDH Interface Type	1595	
Proposed	Frame Relay Service MIB	1604	
Proposed	DNS Server MIB Extensions	1611	
Proposed	DNS Resolver MIB Extensions	1612	
Proposed	UPS Management Information Base	1628	
Standard	Ethernet MIB	1643	50
Draft	BGP-4 MIB	1657	
Draft	Def Man Objs Character Stream	1658	
Draft	Def Man Objs RS-232-like	1659	
Draft	Def Man Objs Parallel-printer-like	1660	
Proposed	SNA NAUs MIB using SMIv2	1666	
Draft	SIP Interface Type MIB	1694	
Proposed	ATM Management Version 8.0 using SMIv2	1695	
Proposed	Modem MIB—Using SMIv2	1696	
Proposed	RDMS MIB—Using SMIv2	1697	
Draft	RIP Version 2 MIB Extension	1724	
Proposed	AppleTalk MIB	1742	
Proposed	SNADLC SDLC MIB Using SMIv2	1747	

Continues

Table 7.2 MIB Documents *(Continued)*

STATUS	NAME	RFC	STD
Draft	IEEE 802.5 Token Ring MIB	1748	
Proposed	802.5 SSR MIB Using SMIv2	1749	
Draft	Remote Network Monitoring MIB	1757	
Proposed	Printer MIB	1759	
Experimental	TCP/IPX Connection MIB Specification	1792	
Draft	OSPF Version 2 MIB	1850	
Draft	Protocol Operations for SNMPv2	1905	
Draft	Transport Mappings for SNMPv2	1906	
Draft	MIB for SNMPv2	1907	
Draft	Coexistence Between SNMPV1 and SNMPV2	1908	
Proposed	Mobile IP MIB Definition Using SMIv2	2006	
Proposed	IEEE 802.12 Interface MIB	2020	
Proposed	RMON MIB Using SMIv2	2021	
Proposed	DLSw MIB Using SMIv2	2024	
Proposed	Entity MIB Using SMIv2	2037	
Proposed	SNANAU APPC MIB Using SMIv2	2051	
Experimental	Traffic Flow Measurement Meter MIB	2064	
Proposed	Remote Network Monitoring MIB	2074	
Proposed	IP Forwarding Table MIB	2096	
Proposed	802.3 Repeater MIB Using SMIv2	2108	
Draft	Management Information Base for Frame	2115	
Proposed	ISDN MIB Using SMIv2	2127	
Proposed	Dial Control MIB using SMIv2	2128	
Proposed	Definitions of Managed Objects for APPN	2155	
Proposed	RSVP Management Information Base	2206	
Proposed	Integrated Services MIB Using SMIv2	2213	
Proposed	Integrated Services MIB Guar Serv Ext	2214	
Proposed	Interfaces Group MIB	2233	
Proposed	Definitions of Managed Objects for HPR	2238	

Table 7.2   *(Continued)*

STATUS	NAME	RFC	STD
Proposed	IEEE 802.3 Medium Attachment Units MIB	2239	
Proposed	Network Services Monitoring MIB	2248	
Proposed	Mail Monitoring MIB	2249	
Proposed	IEEE 802.12 Repeater MIB	2266	
Proposed	Classical IP and ARP over ATM MIB	2320	
Proposed	Ethernet-like Interface Types MIB	2358	
Proposed	Multicast/UNI 3.0/3.1 Based ATM MIB	2417	
Proposed	TCP MIB for IPv6	2452	
Proposed	UDP MIB for IPv6	2454	
Proposed	APPN MIB	2455	
Proposed	APPN TRAPS MIB	2456	
Proposed	Extended Border Node MIB	2457	
Proposed	Textual Conventions, General Group MIB	2465	
Proposed	ICMPv6 Group MIB	2466	
Proposed	DSO MIB/DSOBUNDLE MIB	2494	
Proposed	DS1/E1/DS2/E2 MIB	2495	
Proposed	DS3/E3 Interface Type MIB	2496	
Proposed	Connection-Oriented Accounting MIB	2513	
Proposed	MIB for ATM Management	2515	
Proposed	SONET/SDH Interface Type MIB	2558	
Proposed	TN3270E Using SMIv2 MIB	2561	
Proposed	TN3270E-RT-MIB	2562	
Proposed	Application Management MIB	2564	
Proposed	APPN/HPR in IP Networks MIB	2584	

MIB specifications generally begin with a description of the problem for which they are being proposed as a solution. They also contain a complete, formal definition of the MIB components. This includes ASN.1 representation of the objects defined by the MIB, including a description of the data contained in each object.

The MIB defines what kind of data can be stored and under what object identifier. Devices supporting the MIB are not limited to one instance of any given object. For example, you might want to be able to represent a series of pieces of data all related to a particular entity. In that case, you could use a row to store the related data. You might also want to represent multiple objects containing information about network interfaces for a router or even just a series of instances of a row as in a routing table. Multiple instances of data can be stored in tables, with the table accessible through the object identifier.

Simple Network Management Protocol

The Simple Network Management Protocol (SNMP) actually is quite simple: With IP, it uses a connectionless transport protocol (User Datagram Protocol) that carries data (both requests and replies) in simple message units. The complicated part of the SNMP is the infrastructure: the SMI and MIB structures that all compliant devices and systems must support. Within that infrastructure, which is really just a template for where to store data and what to call it, SNMP operates by sending out a few basic messages.

Two types of entities are defined under SNMP: the agent that sits on every device or system that supports SNMP and the manager, which can send and receive messages to and from agents for the purpose of collecting information about the state of the device and the network in general. There are two basic types of protocol interaction between agents and managers: a request/response interaction, where the manager asks for some information from the agent and the agent replies with the requested information; and the trap, which is sent out unilaterally by an agent when something untoward occurs that the manager might want to know about.

Ethernet-Related MIBs

As we see in more detail in Chapter 14, Ethernet requires several different MIBs, depending on the different ways in which it is used in conjunction with IP. Table 7.3 lists some current MIB specifications for Ethernet. Ethernet must also conform with RFC 2233, "The Interfaces Group MIB using SMIv2."

Table 7.3   RFCs Defining Ethernet-Related MIBs

RFC	TITLE
RFC 2358	Definitions of Managed Objects for the Ethernet-like Interface Types
RFC 1643	Definitions of Managed Objects for the Ethernet-like Interface Types (STD 50)
RFC 2239	Definitions of Managed Objects for IEEE 802.3 Medium Attachment Units (MAUs) Using SMIv2
RFC 2108	Definitions of Managed Objects for IEEE 802.3 Repeater Devices Using SMIv2
RFC 1515	Definitions of Managed Objects for IEEE 802.3 Medium Attachment Units (MAUs)

Reading List

The reader is urged to check out the original RFCs for more information about SNMP, SMI, and MIB. Table 7.4 contains a selection of some documents in this area (other related documents are included in Tables 7.1, 7.2, and 7.3). Marshall Rose, long a key contributor to the ongoing SNMP effort, has written a book that provides an introduction to SNMP and related specifications titled *The Simple Book, 2nd edition* (Prentice Hall, 1996).

Table 7.4   Network Management RFCs

RFC	TITLE
RFC 1155	Structure of Management Information
RFC 1212	Concise MIB Definitions
RFC 1229	Extensions to the Generic-Interface MIB
RFC 1441	Introduction to SNMPv2
RFC 1448	Protocol Operations for SNMPv2
RFC 2570	Introduction to Version 3 of the Internet-standard Network Management Framework
RFC 2572	Message Processing and Dispatching for the Simple Network Management Protocol (SNMP)
RFC 2578	Structure of Management Information Version 2 (SMIv2)

PART

Two

Ethernet Standards

The actual standards that define Ethernet are created outside the IETF: The IEEE develops standards that apply Ethernet technology. However, there are standards and specifications developed within the IETF that rely on, use, or interact with Ethernet and IEEE 802.3 specifications. The rest of this book discusses these specifications.

Chapter 8 starts out with an introduction to Ethernet itself, while Chapter 9 introduces some of the issues raised by attempting to use IP over Ethernet. Chapter 10 explains how the Ethernet Address Resolution Protocol (ARP) and related protocols work, and Chapters 11 and 12 discuss how IPv4 and IPv6, respectively, are transmitted across Ethernet networks. Chapter 13 details transmitting IP multicast and broadcast datagrams across Ethernet networks. Chapter 14 returns to the issues raised in Chapter 7, detailing some of the specifications for managing Ethernet networks using the Simple Network Management Protocol (SNMP) and the Structure of Management Information (SMI). Finally, Chapter 15 provides an overview of the immediate future of Ethernet and IP.

Ethernet Fundamentals

We've been referring to Ethernet as if it were a single type of link layer technology. It is not. Over the years, Ethernet has evolved, branching into several different flavors. The IEEE 802 committee has developed a number of specifications based on Ethernet, and different varieties of Ethernet provide varying bandwidth and network architectures.

We start this chapter with brief look at the history of Ethernet and its related specifications, followed by an overview of the basic Ethernet architecture and design principles. Next, we discuss the different Ethernet and Ethernet-like specifications. The rest of the chapter is devoted to discussion of Ethernet and IEEE 802.3 frames, headers, and trailers as well as IEEE 802 sublayers. We are most interested in how Ethernet and related standards interface with higher-layer protocols (for example, IP) rather than in the electrical characteristics of Ethernet transmissions. The interested reader can find more detailed information about Ethernet elsewhere, for example, *Ethernet Networks, 3rd edition* (Gilbert Held, Wiley Computer Publishing, 1998).

Ethernet History and Background

Work done at the University of Hawaii led by Dr. Norman Abramson during the late 1960s and early 1970s is generally accepted as leading to the birth of Ethernet. This work resulted in the ALOHA network, which used radio transmissions to carry signals from a mainframe to terminals. All transmissions were literally broadcast from mainframe to terminal or terminal to mainframe, with the mainframe sending on one channel and the terminals sharing a second channel. Each channel originally provided only 4800bps, which later increased to 9600bps. Because the terminals shared the sending channel, algorithms for dealing with channel contention were necessary. These formed the basis of packet broadcast systems as we know them, including satellite transmission systems as well as Ethernet.

Dr. Robert Metcalfe, working at the Xerox PARC (Palo Alto Research Center) facility during the 1970s, invented Ethernet by improving the ALOHA work and implementing it over coaxial wire. Metcalfe also named the new technology "Ethernet," after the *ether*, long thought to be the medium through which electromagnetic waves are carried.

This original version of Ethernet provided 2.94Mbps of bandwidth using Carrier-Sense Multiple Access with Collision Detection (CSMA/CD). CSMA/CD describes how Ethernet originally worked. Carrier-sense means that nodes check the carrier to see if the channel is already in use before attempting to send. Multiple access means that more than one node is attached to the network. Collision detection means that nodes attempting to transmit simultaneously are both able to gracefully back off from the collision and transmit their data without undue contention. CSMA/CD has long been fundamental to Ethernets, and a more complete explanation is provided in the next section.

In an effort to turn Ethernet into a product, Xerox initially renamed it Xerox wire. However, cooler heads eventually prevailed. In 1979, Xerox teamed up with Intel and DEC to produce an industry standard for local area connectivity, and the name reverted to Ethernet, also known as DIX Ethernet (for DEC Intel Xerox Ethernet). By 1982, a second version of the standard for Ethernet was published, specifying 10Mbps bandwidth and called variously Ethernet II and Ethernet version 2.0.

In the early 1980s, the IEEE set up its Project 802 to specify standards for office networking technologies. The 802.3 subcommittee was formed to write a standard based on Ethernet. At about the same time, Xerox turned over its patents on Ethernet to the IEEE. Rather than retain the rights to the technology and possibly eke out a portion of a highly fragmented network market, Xerox made possible the development of an open standard that all vendors could use to produce products that interoperate. We revisit the work of the 802.3 group later in this chapter.

Although Ethernet was not the only LAN technology available in the late 1970s and early 1980s, it achieved its prominent position because Metcalfe pushed it as an industry rather than proprietary standard. By cooperating at first with Intel and DEC, and later turning the patents for Ethernet over to the IEEE, Xerox's Ethernet triumphed over competing LAN technologies such as Hyperchannel (from Network Systems Corporation) and ARCnet (from Datapoint). Although these and other LAN technologies are sometimes referred to in RFCs, their significance pales in comparison with Metcalfe's Ethernet.

More recently, advances in Ethernet technology include the movement away from coaxial cables to twisted-pair cabling, increases in bandwidth from 10Mbps to 100Mbps and even to gigabit (1Gbps) networks. We discuss these different Ethernet options later in this chapter.

Basic Ethernet Architecture

We won't be going into all the details of how Ethernet works, and we won't be discussing all the details of the various different types of Ethernet. We won't be weighing the comparative merits of coaxial cabling versus twisted pair or talking about transceivers and signals. Those issues are more relevant to the interface of the link layer protocol to the physical layer of the network; we are more concerned with the interface between the link layer and the network layer (IP). The interested reader is directed to a book like *Ethernet Networks, 3rd edition* (Gilbert Held, Wiley Computer Publishing, 1998) for these details.

Instead of discussing all the different permutations possible with Ethernet, we provide a brief overview to the basic architecture common to almost all types of Ethernet, followed by a general discussion of how Ethernet works as a data communication protocol.

Baseband or Broadband?

LAN media can use either broadband or baseband signaling. With broadband signaling, the signal itself can be divided and shared among more than one sender. The channel is subdivided so that data can be carried from more than one node at a time. Broadband can make possible more efficient use of the channel, but it also tends to be more complicated. Splitting up a signal and multiplexing streams of data means that a recipient must be able to screen out all but its own part of the signal. Special modems are necessary in broadband networks.

Baseband is simpler: Any of the nodes sharing the network can have the entire channel for its transmissions without sharing. When one node is transmitting, no other node can transmit. Nodes must wait for the channel to be clear if they are to successfully transmit packets. However, nodes don't need to do anything special with the signals they receive to filter out irrelevant signals (as with broadband).

Baseband is comparable to a railroad track: If a train is on the track already, you can't put your own train on the track. Broadband is more like a pipeline: You can add your transmission to the flow along the pipe as long as the pipe is not already filled to capacity. However, it can be tricky trying to separate your fluid from the others in the pipeline at any given time.

Almost all Ethernet variations use baseband signaling rather than broadband. Except for 10BROAD36 Ethernet, which allows existing cable access TV (CATV) cables to be adapted for networking use (and has not achieved any significant market acceptance), all Ethernet standards specify baseband signaling.

Carrier-Sense Multiple Access/ Collision Detection (CSMA/CD)

Carrier-Sense Multiple Access/Collision Detection or CSMA/CD succinctly describes Ethernet. The term carrier-sense indicates that nodes check the channel to make sure that no one else is transmitting on it before they attempt to transmit. Multiple access indicates that nodes share the network medium and have access to all network transmissions. Collision detection indicates that, when two nodes have attempted to transmit over the shared network medium at the same time, there is a mechanism for determining which node is transmitted first.

In CSMA/CD networks, a node checks the channel before sending. If there is no traffic for some predetermined amount of time, the node can transmit. If the channel is busy, the node monitors the channel until it is clear and then attempts to transmit. Because another node may have also been monitoring the channel to send, a collision may occur. The node monitors the channel while it is sending so that it can tell when a collision occurs. If it "hears" on the wire only its own transmission, then no collision is occurring. If another transmission is colliding with its own transmission, the two interfere with each other and the sending node detects the problem. At that point, the node sends out a signal indicating that any received packet should be discarded and then waits to send again.

Deciding how long to wait to resend a packet presents a problem: both nodes back off, but only one can send at any given time. If they both back off the same amount of time, they just collide again. A random back-off period is set, so that (it is hoped) the collision does not occur with the same node. In most cases when two nodes are in contention, this is sufficient. The node that backs off for the shortest period of time is able to send its packet. However, if another collision occurs, the node backs off for a longer period before retrying. Collisions are a bigger problem on busy networks than on lightly loaded networks.

CSMA/CD is fundamental to Ethernet running over shared media with a bus architecture. However, the bus architecture is vanishing, superseded in large part by the star topologies that result from cabling all nodes into a single hub or switch. Rather than sharing 10Mbps together, each node has 10Mbps (or 100Mbps or even 1Gbps) of bandwidth direct to the switch. Full-duplex Ethernet, in which each node has two full channels (one for transmitting to the hub and one for receiving packets from the hub), makes CSMA/CD obsolete. Some have argued in favor of removing CSMA/CD from the most recent IEEE specifications for high-speed Ethernets, but it has been retained to allow half-duplex Ethernets, in which only one channel links nodes to the switch. In those cases, the node needs to do carrier-sensing and collision detection to avoid sending when it should be listening to a transmission from the switch.

Ethernet and IEEE 802.3 Protocol Overview

So far, we've mostly used the term Ethernet but in fact there are two separate standards to deal with: the DIX Ethernet v2.0 standard, which has largely been replaced by the IEEE 802.3 standard. As we see in the next section, Ethernet and IEEE 802.3 specifications are very close but not exactly the same. These days, Ethernet II is rarely seen anymore. Usually when someone talks about Ethernet, he or she is actually referring to a network technology specified by an IEEE 802 document.

In the next section, we introduce the standard for Ethernet frames. After that, we look first at the IEEE Project 802 and its committees and then at the standard for IEEE 802.3 frames. After a discussion of IEEE 802 sublayers (IEEE 802.2 and related standards), we finish the chapter with a reading list.

Ethernet Frames

Ethernet defines a mechanism for transmitting data over a network medium. The protocol data unit for Ethernet is the frame: All data transmitted across an Ethernet is encapsulated within a frame. The Ethernet frame itself consists of header fields, payload, and a frame check field at the end. Figure 8.1 shows the basic format for the Ethernet frame. This is the Medium Access Control (MAC) encapsulation, and it represents the data link layer for Ethernet. The MAC contains everything necessary to package up a higher-layer protocol and deliver it on the local link.

Keep in mind that most of the data traveling across what we now call Ethernet is encapsulated within IEEE 802.3 frames rather than the Ethernet frames shown here. We discuss the Ethernet frame structure here to provide an understanding of the protocol and for background. We examine the 802.3 frame later in the chapter.

The basic fields of an Ethernet frame include the following:

Preamble field. This 8-byte sequence is not strictly speaking a field. It simply identifies the start of all Ethernet frames. The preamble field acts as a synchronization tool. It consists of a sequence of 62 bits of alternating 1s and 0s (starting out 10101010101 and continuing for 62 bits), ending with two bits both set to 1 (...10101011) to indicate that an Ethernet frame is about to start.

Destination address field. This 6-byte field consists of the Ethernet media access control (MAC) or hardware address of the Ethernet interface to which the frame is being sent (see sidebar on MAC addresses below).

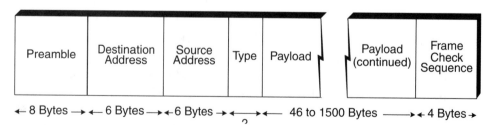

Figure 8.1   The Ethernet frame.

Source address field. This 6-byte field consists of the Ethernet MAC address of the Ethernet interface from which the frame is being sent.

Type field. This 2-byte field contains an EtherType value, indicating the protocol used for the frame payload. This value is always greater than 1500 decimal (we see why when we discuss the IEEE 802.3 frame) and is 0x0800 for IPv4 packets and 0x86dd for IPv6 packets.

The payload. Ethernet payloads can be anywhere from 46 to 1500 bytes. The payload carries a higher-layer protocol's packet, such as an IPv4 or IPv6 datagram.

The frame check sequence (FCS) or cyclic redundancy check (CRC). This four-byte field consists of the result of a mathematical operation performed on the data in the frame by the sender. The receiving node repeats the operation on the frame, and if the value it calculates matches the value of the CRC, the frame is processed. Otherwise, the recipient requests that the frame be resent.

The minimum size of the Ethernet frame payload is 46 bytes and the maximum is 1500 bytes. We revisit issues related to the maximum length of the payload later in this chapter as well as later in the book. When the protocol payload being encapsulated and transmitted over Ethernet is smaller than 46 bytes, padding bits (all zeros) are required to create a frame that is 64 bytes long, exclusive of the preamble. The frame consists of a 6-byte destination address + 6-byte source address + 2-byte EtherType + payload (greater than or equal to 46) + 4-byte CRC = 64 bytes (or more).

ETHERNET HARDWARE ADDRESSES

There's not much point to having a network in which you can not uniquely identify nodes: How else could you send data to its intended destination? The Media Access Control (MAC) address is a value associated with the physical network interface. For Ethernet, this usually means a 48-bit value hard-coded into the network interface card or device that attaches the node to the network.

Ethernet MAC addresses are intended to be globally unique, with blocks of address space allocated to Ethernet device vendors. The first three bytes of the address identify the vendor, while the last three bytes of the address uniquely identify the device within that vendor's production.

Cases of duplicate MAC addresses have been reported for very inexpensive Ethernet interface cards, and some operating systems permit the manual configuration of a MAC address, but otherwise MAC address collisions should not normally occur.

IEEE 802 Standards

The IEEE Project 802, also dubbed the "Local Network Standards Committee," first met in February of 1980, hence its name (the first two digits, 80, refer to the year while the last digit indicates the month of February). Now also known as the LAN/MAN Standards Committee (LMSC), IEEE Project 802 develops standards for local area networks (LANs, which are networks that span but not go beyond a "campus") and metropolitan area networks (MANs, which are networks that can span but not go beyond a city), concentrating on the lowest two layers of the OSI reference model (the physical and data link layers).

Originally, the intent for the project was to base standards on the Ethernet access method with a bus topology. By the end of 1980, the project was studying both the bus and token ring topologies with three medium access control types: Ethernet CSMA/CD, token bus, and token ring. CSMA/CD work was assigned to the 802.3 working group, token bus to the 802.4 group, and token ring to the 802.5 group. These groups define standards for the physical layer.

Other groups were chartered for other types of network access, including wireless and cable TV. The IEEE 802.2 working group was set up to define standards for the link layer. One of its specifications was for the Logical Link Control (LLC) standard, which is the protocol used to format networking frames in such a way as to map frames onto upper-layer protocols (such as IP). LLC represents a sublayer of the data link layer. We return to IEEE 802.2 later in this section as well as later in the book when we discuss how IP packets are encapsulated within Ethernet frames.

The Ethernet naming convention uses the form "nTYPE-m" where n is the bandwidth of the network in Mbps, TYPE is either BASE (for baseband signaling) or BROAD (for broadband signaling), and m represents the maximum segment length in meters. The type of Ethernet we have come to consider the "standard" is 10Mbps, carried over unshielded twisted pair cable to a hub, also known as 10BASE-T—an exception to the naming rule. In fact, the convention increasingly uses letters to indicate a type of Ethernet medium instead of maximum segment length, resulting in things like 100BASE-T (Fast Ethernet over unshielded twisted pair) and 100BASE-FX (Fast Ethernet over fiber).

The original Ethernet, as described in Metcalfe and D. Boggs' article "Ethernet: Distributed Packet Switching for Local Computer Networks" published in the Communications of the ACM (V.19, N.7, pp. 395-402,

July 1976) had 3Mbps of bandwidth (actually, 2.94Mbps) and used 8-bit addresses. An Internet standard exists for running IP over this experimental Ethernet: STD 42 (RFC 895) "A Standard for the Transmission of IP Datagrams over Experimental Ethernet Networks." However, the standard for running IP over regular Ethernet is defined by STD 41 (RFC 894) "A Standard for the Transmission of IP Datagrams over Ethernet Networks."

Ethernet can run over a variety of network media and at several different bandwidths. The specifics and differences between these different incarnations are not as important to us as the link layer framing common to all Ethernet variations and the way in which Ethernet interacts with IP.

IEEE 802.3 Frames

An IEEE 802.3 frame looks very much like an Ethernet frame, as can be seen by comparing the IEEE 802.3 format shown in Figure 8.2 with the Ethernet frame format shown in Figure 8.1. The first difference appears in the preamble. Instead of an 8-byte preamble, as in Ethernet, IEEE 802.3 uses a 7-byte preamble consisting of alternating 1s and 0s and a 1-byte Start of Frame Delimiter, consisting of the sequence "10101011." This is, of course, exactly the same as the Ethernet 8-byte preamble in everything except name.

Another difference between 802.3 and Ethernet is that 802.3 allows either 2-byte or 6-byte MAC addresses. Though you will be hard-pressed to find any 16-bit Ethernet addresses nowadays, they were allowed in the specification for compatibility with network interfaces manufactured around the same time the standards were written, which was the early 1980s. With 6-byte addresses, the IEEE 802.3 frame and the Ethernet frame are so far functionally identical, and thus both types

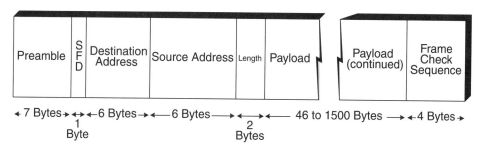

Figure 8.2 The IEEE 802.3 frame.

of frames can coexist on the same network. Also identical for both IEEE 802.3 and Ethernet is the limit on the size of the frame payload of no less than 46 bytes and no more than 1500 bytes as well as the frame check sequence (FCS) field.

The only significant difference between IEEE 802.3 and Ethernet frames is in the field just before the payload. For Ethernet, this is the EtherType field. For IEEE 802.3, however, this field is used to indicate the length of the payload, and its value can be equal to or greater than 46 but no higher than 1500.

The EtherType/length field represents a bar to IEEE 802.3 and Ethernet being interoperable, but it does not prevent Ethernet and IEEE 802.3 frames from coexisting on the same network. Valid EtherTypes must be greater than 1500 (decimal), and the maximum length of an IEEE 802.3 payload is 1500. A node can determine whether a frame is an Ethernet or IEEE 802.3 frame simply by testing whether the EtherType/length field is greater than 1500.

The lack of an EtherType field in the IEEE 802.3 frame leads to a problem: How can a network stack determine what to do with a frame unless it knows the higher layer protocol of the payload? This is where the IEEE 802.2 standards come into play: the Logical Link Control (LLC) sublayer and the Sub-Network Access Protocol (SNAP). We look at both of these in the next section.

IEEE 802.2

Ethernet II provided a link layer protocol with its MAC encapsulation. The destination and source addresses, coupled with the EtherType of the encapsulated protocol, are sufficient for a node to process an Ethernet frame. The node can tell whether it is the intended destination of the frame, and it can also determine what to do with the encapsulated data (by checking the EtherType to see what stack to pass the data to) once it strips off the Ethernet headers and trailer.

However, the IEEE 802.3 (and 802.4 and 802.5, for that matter) standards define the physical layer characteristics of Ethernet, including how the signaling is done and how the frames are transmitted. The addresses and the length of the frame—the data included in the IEEE 802.3 specification—are not enough information for a node to know how to process the frame.

The IEEE 802.2 standards define the data link layer characteristics of LAN networks. IEEE 802.2 framing is applied to the local area network data, in effect linking the data being signaled across the physical layer with the data being manipulated by the higher-layer protocols such as IP. The Logical Link Control (LLC) protocol defines a mechanism to identify the source and destination Service Access Points (SSAP and DSAP) for the encapsulated payload. This mechanism, though useful for some applications, is not sufficient for interoperable use with IP. The Sub-Network Access Protocol (SNAP) must be used with LLC when the frame carries an IP datagram, as we see next.

Logical Link Control (LLC)

LLC adds a set of header fields to the IEEE 802.3 (or other network protocol) headers. The LLC headers are part of the payload of the LAN frame, as shown in Figure 8.3. LLC uses the notion of Service Access Point (SAP) to represent a sort of delivery or pickup point for network data. Nodes know what to do with data that has been received by looking up the destination SAP. SAP values are pointers

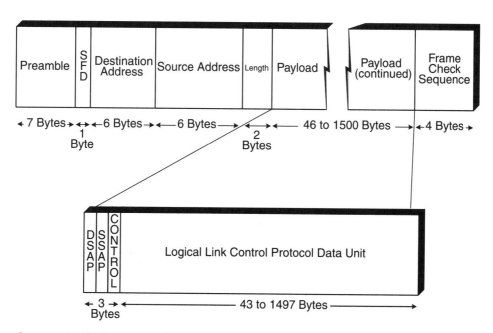

Figure 8.3 The IEEE 802.3 frame with LLC encapsulation.

that may indicate a network protocol such as Novell NetWare, Banyan VINES, or NetBIOS.

The fields in the LLC header include:

Destination SAP (DSAP). This is a one-byte field containing data that identifies the SAP for which the encapsulated data is intended.

Source SAP (SSAP). This is a one-byte field containing data that identifies the SAP from which the encapsulated data was sent.

Control field. This one- or two-byte field carries information relating to LLC commands, responses, and frame sequencing. Contents vary depending on context.

Information field. This is the payload encapsulated within the LLC frame.

Technically, the payload of the physical layer frame (the part labeled payload in Figure 8.2) contains an LLC protocol data unit (LPDU) when LLC is being used. The IEEE 802.3 frame encapsulates an LLC frame or LPDU, which in turn encapsulates something else (we get to that next).

The problem with LLC is that the SAP structure does not map cleanly onto the EtherType space. IP nodes need to be able to pass the frame payload on to the appropriate protocol. With SAPs, the node keeps track of the source and destination applications that generate the frames, but those values won't necessarily be retained as the IP packet moves across different networks on its way to its ultimate destination. The EtherType is a necessity for IP, and the Sub-Network Access Protocol (SNAP) is designed to extend LLC to carry EtherTypes.

Sub-Network Access Protocol (SNAP)

IEEE 802.3/LLC frames use SNAP to encapsulate the IP packets (or any other upper-layer protocol that requires EtherType values in the link layer protocol). A SNAP frame is encapsulated within the LLC frame, as shown in Figure 8.4. The LLC headers for SNAP frames are as follows:

DSAP 170 (decimal) or 0xAA (hex).

SSAP 170 (decimal) or 0xAA (hex).

Control field 3 (indicating unnumbered information in the payload).

These values indicate that the first five bytes of the LLC payload are actually used for the two SNAP headers:

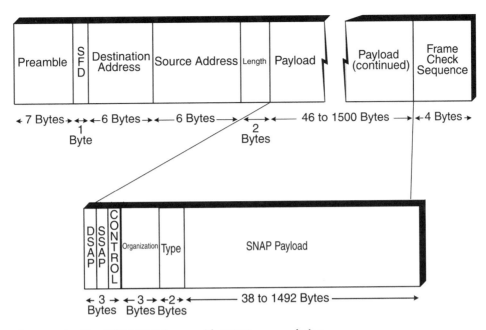

Figure 8.4 The IEEE 802.3 frame with SNAP encapsulation.

Organization code. A three-byte field indicating the organization responsible for administering the values found in the Type field. For EtherTypes, this value is set to 0.

Type. A two-byte field containing the EtherType of the protocol encapsulated within the SNAP frame. This field could contain any two-byte type identifier, depending on the value of the organization code.

It is worth noting that the LLC and SNAP headers reduce the size of the payload possible in an IEEE 802.3 fame by eight bytes. The maximum frame size continues to be 1518 bytes (1500 payload + 14 MAC header + 4 FCS), but the maximum actual payload is only 1492 bytes because eight bytes of the payload are devoted to LLC/SNAP headers.

Reading List

Ethernet and IEEE standards are defined outside of the IETF. There are no RFCs that discuss these protocols on their own. Table 8.1 contains a list of some Web sites with useful information about these standards. In addition to the IEEE and Gigabit Ethernet Forum, your favorite network product vendor probably also has information online about Ethernet.

Table 8.1 Web Sites with Ethernet/IEEE Standard Information

URL	ORGANIZATION	DESCRIPTION
http://standards.ieee.org/	IEEE	Web site for IEEE standards; you can freely view certain working group activities but must pay to download actual standards (including the IEEE 802.3 standards).
http://grouper.ieee.org/ groups/802/index.html	IEEE 802 LAN/MAN Standards Committee	Information about the creation and development of local/metropolitan area networking standards by IEEE.
http://www.gigabit-Ethernet.org	Gigabit Ethernet Forum	Provides some technical and industry information about gigabit Ethernet.

CHAPTER 9

Internet Standards and Ethernet

It is overly glib to state that interfacing a link layer protocol with a network layer protocol, similar to the interface between Ethernet and IP that we are discussing here, is a simple matter. Even if the interface between Ethernet and IP is relatively straightforward, other link layer protocols, such as ATM, can present significant difficulties (see *Essential ATM Standards: RFCs and Protocols Made Practical*, by Pete Loshin, John Wiley & Sons, 1999).

Mapping IP onto a link layer protocol requires specifying several different issues: How does one map an IP address to a link layer address? How does one encapsulate IP datagrams into the link layer protocol data unit? How does one transmit broadcast and multicast packets over the link layer? How does one manage link layer network devices via IP? In this chapter, we clarify the problems related to each of these categories and discuss, in very general terms, the solutions being standardized for use of IP over Ethernet.

Address Resolution

Link layer network addresses are the addresses that identify a node's network interface to the physical medium of the local link. The addresses themselves are usually either hard-coded into the network interface hardware or are assigned through some process that is independent of the upper protocol layers.

This means that there is no simple and straightforward mechanism that maps an upper-layer protocol address (such as an IP address) to the link layer address. Link layer addresses and network layer addresses are usually incompatible in the extreme. Although it is possible to manually map IP addresses onto a table of link layer addresses, this approach scales quite poorly as networks grow and is prone to problems as nodes change their locations and hardware over time.

Plainly, what is necessary is a mechanism that allows nodes to figure out where to send link layer frames once they've determined a destination's IP address. Ethernet address resolution is done under IPv4 (as well as other network layer protocols) through the mechanism defined in RFC 826, "An Ethernet Address Resolution Protocol—or—Converting Network Protocol Addresses to 48.bit Ethernet Address for Transmission on Ethernet Hardware." As we see in Chapter 10, the Address Resolution Protocol (ARP) has been extended and adapted not just to add functionality over Ethernet networks but also to be used in both broadcast and nonbroadcast link layer networks.

IPv4 over Ethernet

Finding a way to map IP addresses to Ethernet addresses is an important part of running IP over Ethernet, but not the only part. There are other issues to deal with, and the existence of two distinct standards for Ethernet (the Ethernet II specification and the IEEE 802.3 specification) means that the waters can be a little muddier than would otherwise be expected.

Several issues must be dealt with, and these are discussed in Chapter 11. First, guidelines must be given for the proper way to encapsulate IP in Ethernet/IEEE 802.3 frames. Also, consideration must be given to the issue of how best to format IP packets—how big should they be, for example. The maximum transmission unit (MTU) size of the link layer network (Ethernet) makes a difference for IP, as we see when we discuss

Ethernet, Path MTUs, and packet fragmentation. We also discuss how IEEE 802.2 LLC and SNAP headers are applied to IPv4.

No discussion of IP over a link layer protocol can be complete without discussion of broadcast and multicast issues. We discuss these in Chapter 13.

IPv6 over Ethernet

One of the biggest issues related to doing IP over any link layer—that is, address resolution—changes drastically with IPv6, the next revision of the Internet Protocol. Although ARP is not supported for IPv6, new mechanisms for neighbor discovery and address configuration are defined for IPv6 that make ARP obsolete.

In Chapter 12, we look at the proposed standard for transmitting IPv6 over Ethernet, RFC 2464, "Transmission of IPv6 Packets over Ethernet Networks." This RFC discusses the mechanisms to be used for encapsulating IPv6 in Ethernet, MTU issues, and especially issues related to neighbor discovery and the IEEE 64-bit Global Identifier (EUI-64).

Multicast, Broadcast, and Ethernet

Broadcast has long been an important part of IP, and multicast is growing in significance. Both are easy to specify for network layer protocols like IP but are not always as easy to implement in the data link and physical layers. Ethernet provides a relatively supportive environment for point-to-multipoint (broadcast and multicast) transmissions. Chapter 13 examines STD 5, which encompasses three RFCs: RFC 919, "Broadcasting Internet Datagrams"; RFC 922, "Broadcasting Internet Datagrams in the Presence of Subnets"; and RFC 1112, "Host Extensions for IP Multicasting (IGMP)." Also covered are issues addressed in proposed standards RFC 2362, "Protocol Independent Multicast-Sparse Mode (PIM-SM): Protocol Specification," and RFC 1584, "Multicast Extensions to OSPF."

Ethernet and Network Management

As discussed in Chapter 7, network devices need to be managed, and the SNMP, SMI, and MIB frameworks provide an excellent foundation for managing network (link layer) devices through the network (IP) layer. In Chapter 14, we introduce the MIBs defined for managing Ethernet devices with SNMP.

Ethernet Address
Resolution Protocol

Early RFCs seem to have had a bit less quality control than modern ones. RFC 826, "An Ethernet Address Resolution Protocol—or—Converting Network Protocol Addresses to 48.bit Ethernet Address for Transmission on Ethernet Hardware," is a good example of a nonstandard standard. Though the author specifically proclaims that the mechanism described in RFC 826 is not intended to be an Internet standard, it has become one (it is now STD-37). In part because Ethernet ARP was documented as a request for comments in the original sense of being an offering of a possible solution to a well-known problem, the RFC itself is not as clear and readable as many later RFCs that have been subjected to numerous rewrites as well as extensive editorial scrutiny.

The Address Resolution Protocol (ARP), originally described as a mechanism for 10Mbps Ethernet, has been expanded and generalized in several different ways over the years and has become a very important mechanism for all IP implementations. In this chapter, we concentrate on the basic ARP protocol as it is applied to Ethernet (and as described in RFC 826), followed by a brief discussion of related address resolution protocols such as the Reverse Address Resolution Protocol (RARP), Inverse Address Resolution Protocol (InARP), and others.

The Address Resolution Problem

Networks depend on addresses to make sure that data can get from a source to a destination. An Ethernet is a network, and though it may carry IP network traffic, it is not able to directly use IP network addresses (any more than IP can use Ethernet network addresses). A mechanism must be in place to map internetwork layer protocol addresses to link layer protocol addresses.

A number of approaches address the problem of mapping link layer addresses to network layer addresses, some more sensible than others. A very obvious one is to manually configure each node with a table containing all Ethernet (MAC) and IP addresses on the local link. Just as obviously, this approach is flawed: It is highly labor-intensive and becomes even more so as nodes are moved, added, and removed from the LAN.

Another approach is to have each node periodically broadcast its network layer address to the LAN and have each node on the network keep a table of broadcast values. This is a better solution as it requires no manual configuration and has the advantage of being continuously updated. On the down side, however, this approach creates a background of address advertisement broadcasts that detract from overall LAN bandwidth. In addition, nodes must keep track of and maintain timers on all the other nodes in the LAN. When a node goes off the LAN (for example, is powered off for the night), other nodes must be able to recognize that the broadcasts have stopped and thus infer that the node is unreachable.

The best solution turns out to use broadcasts in a more efficient manner. When a node wants to reach another node, it can broadcast a request for address resolution information. The destination node can unicast back the answer to the requesting node. This keeps the noise to a minimum and relieves nodes of the duty to track each other all the time, even if they never need to communicate.

This is, in a nutshell, the way the Ethernet Address Resolution Protocol (ARP) works. Each node on an Ethernet LAN listens for address resolution requests, and if the address being requested belongs to the node, it must respond with its MAC address.

Although it was devised to allow network layer protocols (most notably IP) to resolve link layer addresses on Ethernet LANs, ARP can be used by any network layer protocol (DECnet, CHAOS, and Xerox PUP are cited in RFC 826) to resolve addresses for many types of link layer protocols. As we see later, ARP has even been adapted for use in networks that don't support broadcasts.

Overview to the ARP Mechanism

ARP is quite a simple protocol. It is carried within Ethernet frames and uses a single format for all messages. Because ARP is extensible to many different network and link layer protocols, it contains fields that identify the network layer protocol and the link layer protocol address spaces in use. Because protocol addresses can be of different lengths, fields indicate the length of the link layer protocol addresses and the network layer protocol addresses. (The Ethernet MAC address of course is 48 bits, or 6 bytes, and the IP address is 32 bits, or 4 bytes.) Finally, there are four address fields: the link layer and network layer addresses of the source node (the node sending the ARP message) and the link layer and network layer addresses of the destination node (the node that is the target of the ARP message).

When a node needs to send a network layer packet to a network layer destination—in other words, the IP source wants to send an IP packet to a destination—the sender does what it needs as far as routing and then checks a table to see if it has a link layer address for that destination. If it does, away the packet goes, encapsulated inside an Ethernet frame. If not, the sender needs to get a link layer address.

This works quite simply: The originating node sends out an ARP request. This request contains all the appropriate information about network layer and link layer protocols, address sizes, and the link layer and network layer address of the sender, and the network layer address of the destination. The link layer address field is left out. The whole thing is identified as a request by an operation code and is broadcast to the local Ethernet.

Now, every time a node on an Ethernet receives a broadcast ARP request, it checks the contents of the message. If the recipient has the same IP address as the IP address in the target network layer field, then the recipient knows it must respond. A response is generated by taking the ARP request, putting the source link layer and network layer addresses in the destination fields, putting the destination network layer field in the source field, and filling the source field with the recipient's link layer address. Finally, the operation code is changed to indicate the ARP message is a reply. The new message is sent back as a unicast Ethernet frame, rather than a broadcast, and the node that requested the address resolution can now address IP packets to an Ethernet address.

ARP Messages

The ARP message format is shown in Figure 10.1. This message is encapsulated within an Ethernet frame, which is the destination MAC address followed by the source MAC address and protocol type. The fields within the ARP message are listed below. The field names are taken from RFC 826. Instead of "link layer" and "network layer," the RFC uses the terms "hardware" and "protocol." The fields include the following:

Hardware address space. This is a two-byte value that indicates the protocol in use. As of 1999, 28 different values were recognized for this field. Table 10.2 is taken from the IANA Web site and lists the values. The important values for our purposes are 1, which represents 10Mb Ethernet, and 6, which represents IEEE 802 networks.

Protocol address space. This two-byte field contains an EtherType, a value that identifies the type of protocol encapsulated within an Eth-

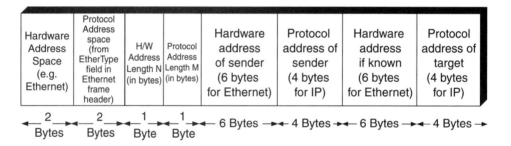

```
From RFC 826:
Ethernet packet data:
        16.bit: (ar$hrd) Hardware address space (e.g., Ethernet,
                         Packet Radio Net.)
        16.bit: (ar$pro) Protocol address space.  For Ethernet
                         hardware, this is from the set of type
                         fields ether_typ$<protocol>.
         8.bit: (ar$hln) byte length of each hardware address
         8.bit: (ar$pln) byte length of each protocol address
        16.bit: (ar$op)  opcode (ares_op$REQUEST | ares_op$REPLY)
        nbytes: (ar$sha) Hardware address of sender of this
                         packet, n from the ar$hln field.
        mbytes: (ar$spa) Protocol address of sender of this
                         packet, m from the ar$pln field.
        nbytes: (ar$tha) Hardware address of target of this
                         packet (if known).
        mbytes: (ar$tpa) Protocol address of target.
```

Figure 10.1 The ARP message format.

ernet frame. IANA maintains an unofficial list of EtherTypes, which are maintained officially by the IEEE. For our purposes, the only relevant EtherTypes are 0x0800, for IPv4, and 0x86DD, for IPv6.

Length of hardware address (in bytes). This one-byte field contains the length, in bytes, of the hardware addresses being resolved. Thus, an address space supporting up to 255 byte addresses could be supported through ARP. Ethernet uses 48-bit or six-byte addresses.

Length of protocol address (in bytes). This one-byte field contains the length, in bytes, of the protocol addresses being resolved. For IPv4, the value is 4 (IPv4 uses 32-bit addresses).

Operation code. This two-byte field contains a code indicating the type of ARP message. Close to two dozen operation codes have been specified, according to the IANA Web site. Table 10.1 lists the values specific to ARP and related protocols and documented in RFCs. It also references the sources where they are documented.

Source hardware address. This field contains the link layer address of the node originating the ARP message. This field is of variable length, but for our purposes, it is always six bytes long and contains an Ethernet MAC address.

Source protocol address. This field contains the network layer address of the node originating the ARP message. This field is also of variable length, but for our purposes, it is always four bytes long and contains an IPv4 address.

Destination hardware address. This field contains the destination link layer MAC address. For requests, this might contain a broadcast address—all ones on an Ethernet. However, the actual destination address of the ARP message is set in the Ethernet frame, so there is no need to set it here too for an ARP Request.

Destination protocol address. This field contains the destination network layer (IP) address. This field contains the IP address that must be resolved to a link layer address for ARP Requests.

ARP messages are treated differently, depending on the operation code they carry. RFC 826 defines only two opcodes: 1 indicating a Request and 2 indicating a Reply. Other variant protocols that use ARP messages include Reverse ARP (RARP), Dynamic Reverse ARP (DRARP), and Inverse ARP (InARP). These are discussed later in this chapter. Table 10.1 lists opcodes that are defined by RFCs for the ARP message.

Table 10.1   ARP Operation Codes

OPERATION CODE	VALUE	SOURCE
REQUEST	1	RFC 826
REPLY	2	RFC 826
Request Reverse	3	RFC 903
Reply Reverse	4	RFC 903
DRARP-Request	5	RFC 1931
DRARP-Reply	6	RFC 1931
DRARP-Error	7	RFC 1931
InARP-Request	8	RFC 2390
InARP-Reply	9	RFC 2390

An ARP Request message is sent to the Ethernet broadcast address (all-ones). The source MAC address and broadcast destination address are placed in the Ethernet frame header. The value placed in the destination address field inside the ARP Request message is not important to the protocol, so it does not really matter what gets put there.

As is evidenced by the number of different hardware types that have been specified for it, ARP is a popular mechanism for resolving link layer addresses from IP addresses. Table 10.2 lists values for this field that are taken from the IANA Web site.

Table 10.2   ARP Hardware Types (adapted from www.IANA.org)

HARDWARE TYPE	VALUE
Ethernet (10Mb)	1
Experimental Ethernet (3Mb)	2
Amateur Radio AX.25	3
Proteon ProNET Token Ring	4
Chaos	5
IEEE 802 Networks	6
ARCNET	7
Hyperchannel	8
Lanstar	9
Autonet Short Address	10

Table 10.2   *(Continued)*

HARDWARE TYPE	VALUE
LocalTalk	11
LocalNet (IBM PCNet or SYTEK LocalNET)	12
Ultra link	13
SMDS	14
Frame Relay	15
Asynchronous Transfer Mode (ATM)	16
HDLC	17
Fibre Channel	18
Asynchronous Transfer Mode (ATM)	19
Serial Line	20
Asynchronous Transfer Mode (ATM)	21
MIL-STD-188-220	22
Metricom	23
IEEE 1394.1995	24
MAPOS	25
Twinaxial	26
EUI-64	27
HIPARP	28

Protocol Activity for ARP

ARP is independent of IP: It will work with any network layer protocol. The network layer protocol determines a packet's destination, generates the packet and packet headers, and passes the packet on down the protocol stack. At some point, some mechanism within the node's network stack determines that there is a packet destined for the network and that it will be necessary to encapsulate that packet within a link layer frame. At that point, the mechanism consults an address resolution table to see if the network layer address is associated with a link layer address. If so, the network stack can encapsulate the packet within a link layer frame, address the frame to the link layer address indicated for the network layer address, and go merrily on its way.

However, if the network layer address is not listed on that table, then (according to RFC 826) the mechanism might throw the packet away and send notification up the stack that the packet has been discarded. Some protocol at a higher layer eventually resends the data, but in the meantime, the address resolution mechanism must set about resolving the address to a local link address.

Generating an ARP Request

The first step is to generate an ARP request message. This message indicates the EtherType of the network layer protocol (0x0800 for IPv4), the hardware address type (a value from Table 10.2, most probably "1" for 10Mbps Ethernet or "6" for IEEE 802 networks), and hardware and protocol (link layer and network layer) address lengths of six bytes for Ethernet and four bytes for IPv4. (If you were to use ARP for IPv6, it would take a 16 for that field, but IPv6 does not use ARP, as we see in Chapter 12.)

The rest of the ARP request message is formed by putting the node's own Ethernet MAC address in the source hardware address field, the node's own IP address in the source protocol address field, and the destination's IP address in the destination protocol address field. As has already been mentioned, the destination hardware address of an ARP request is ignored. RFC 826 notes that putting the link layer broadcast address in that field could be useful for some implementations, but it is not necessary.

Once the ARP request has been generated, it is broadcast on the local link. When the ARP request has flown, all the nodes on the link receive it and process it.

Receiving an ARP Message

When a node receives an ARP request, the receiving node processes it by examining the different fields in the message. RFC 826 describes the process as asking a sequence of questions about the ARP message. There are no assumptions made about whether the message is an ARP request or a reply. All ARP messages can be processed in the same order, looking at the data in the message first and then looking at the operation code indicating the type of message.

The first question that must be answered is whether the recipient supports the hardware addresses indicated in the hardware address space field. Assuming that the value in this field is correct (that is, that it refers to the actual link layer protocol being used), the receiving node virtually always supports the hardware address space indicated. The node might also verify that the hardware address length contains an expected value. If the hardware address space field indicates an Ethernet (6 byte) address but the hardware address length field indicates some other value, the recipient can discard the message as flawed.

The next step is to examine the EtherType specified in the protocol address field. If the recipient node's network stack supports the protocol specified, then the message continues. However, if the protocol is not supported on that node, the receiving node can safely discard the message. For example, a node running only IP over Ethernet can safely ignore an ARP request for an IPX or DECnet address mapping. The node may also do a sanity check on the expected protocol address length field.

If it is a protocol that the node supports, the next step is to check whether the pairing of <protocol type, sender protocol address> already exists in the address resolution table. RFC 826 also indicates that a merge flag should be set to equal False (this allows the address resolution table to be updated if necessary). If the sender's protocol address is in the resolution table, the table should be updated with the new address information (the data contained in the current ARP message), and the merge flag is set to True.

Note that the recipient of an ARP message checks to see if it already knows about the sender before even checking what kind of ARP message has been sent. In this way, every time an ARP request message is broadcast to the local link, all nodes will update their address resolution table for the node making the request. When a node receives an ARP reply, the node first updates its resolution table for the node sending the request, eliminating the need for the recipient node to send its own ARP request when its upper-layer protocol or application sends a response to that node.

The next step in processing the ARP message is to determine whether the receiving node has the protocol address that the requesting node is looking for. In other words, is the node the destination of the ARP request? If it is, then it—and only it—can send off an ARP reply message. First, however, it must check to see if the merge flag is still set to false. If so, the requesting node is not already in the destination node's address resolution table, and it should be: The fact that the node is requesting address resolution information for the node almost certainly means the requesting node will be sending data to the destination node very soon. This will very likely require the destination node to respond to that data, so having an address mapping from IP address to MAC address is very useful.

At that point, the receiving node puts the triplet <protocol type, sender protocol address, sender hardware address> in its address resolution table, and only then does the receiving node check to see what the message's opcode is. If the opcode indicates the ARP message is a request (and if the receiving node is the destination, and if it supports the hardware and protocol address types specified in the ARP message), then the recipient node has to put its own IP and MAC addresses in the source address fields, put the requesting node's addresses in the destination IP and MAC address fields, change the opcode field to a 2 to indicate an ARP reply message, and unicast the message to the requesting node.

The node making the original request receives the ARP reply and goes through the same process, updating its address resolution table by adding the <protocol type, sender protocol address, sender hardware address> of the node it was querying. After updating the table, when the recipient of the reply determines that the message actually is an ARP reply and not a response, the node simply discards the message without any further action. It can now encapsulate IP packets within Ethernet frames addressed directly to the destination node.

Extending ARP

Address resolution is a very important function when there is a disjoint between link layer network addresses and network layer network addresses. There are more address resolution problems than the simple one of mapping a destination IP address to a MAC address. In this section, we look at several variations on ARP: Reverse ARP, Gratuitous ARP, Inverse ARP, Dynamic RARP, Directed ARP, NBMA, and ATM ARP. Some of these have proven useful enough to become part of standards-track RFCs. Others are documented as experimental. Although RARP is an Internet standard, several, including gratuitous ARP, are proposed standards. RARP and gratuitous ARP are most important for Ethernet networks; the rest are of interest as related protocols, and some are not even used over Ethernets. We begin this section with a discussion of RARP and gratuitous ARP and follow it with a summary of the other ARP variations.

RARP

ARP was designed so that nodes on a network could find out a link layer address associated with a network layer address. RFC 903 (STD 38), "Reverse Address Resolution Protocol," describes a different sort of problem: How can a node discover its own IP address, given that it already knows its MAC address? Diskless workstations, especially 15 or 20 years ago, haven't always encoded IP configurations on board, but may need to get their boot configuration from the network. Reverse ARP (RARP) provides a mechanism to achieve this goal. RARP can also be used in any case in which a node has a link layer address but needs to know what network layer address is associated with it.

With RARP as with the original ARP, a broadcast network medium such as Ethernet is assumed. However, unlike in ARP, RARP distinguishes between a client node (a node requiring RARP services) and a server node (a node providing RARP services). The RARP server listens on the local link for RARP requests (ARP opcode = 3, indicating a reverse request), while RARP clients—the diskless workstations—send these requests out on the link layer broadcast address.

The requesting node sends out a broadcast frame containing the RARP reverse request message. This message contains the link layer address of the requesting node (as the source hardware address) as well as the link layer address that is being requested from a network layer address. The protocol addresses for both source and destination are not defined. For the diskless workstation, this means that the hardware address of both the source and destination will be its own MAC address, and the IP address fields will be undefined.

All nodes on the network receive these RARP requests, but only a RARP server responds. The RARP server maintains a mapping of IP and MAC addresses, and when it receives a RARP request, it responds by filling out the ARP message with the MAC address of the requesting node as the destination along with the IP address associated with that address.

Even though it uses the same ARP message format, RARP is distinguished from ARP as a separate protocol with its own EtherType (ARP is 0x0806 while RARP uses 0x0835). This allows nodes that support ARP (which should be all IP nodes) but not RARP to ignore RARP messages.

Proxy ARP and Gratuitous ARP

RFC 2002, "IP Mobility Support," is a proposed standard that describes several different mechanisms useful for transparent routing of packets to and from mobile IP nodes. Two of these mechanisms involve ARP: Proxy ARP and gratuitous ARP. It turns out that these mechanisms are useful not just for mobile nodes but for regular nodes as well.

Proxy ARP uses a proxy system that acts on behalf of a node that can not respond for itself to ARPs. For example, in a bridged Ethernet, broadcasts are not always forwarded across the bridge. This means that nodes on one side of the bridge can not respond to ARP requests sent by nodes on the other side of the bridge. The Proxy ARP server keeps track of MAC and IP address mappings and responds to ARP requests on behalf of those nodes for which it serves as proxy.

Gratuitous ARP is the term used to describe a mechanism by which nodes send out ARP requests for their own IP and MAC addresses to cause all other nodes to update their ARP caches. The idea is to have nodes send out these broadcasts whenever they rejoin the network. It turns out that this works for nodes that are not mobile but that frequently disappear from the LAN, such as personal computers that drop off the network every night when they are powered down. Most IP implementations generate the gratuitous ARP request when the system is booted up. Depending on how it is implemented, gratuitous ARP can be helpful in determining whether another host is currently using the same IP address. (We discuss this issue again in Chapter 15 when we cover some work being done to address this problem directly.)

InARP

At times and in certain types of networks—notably Frame Relay and related networks—a node knows the link layer address for another node but not the IP address for that node. RFC 2390, "Inverse Address Resolution Protocol," is a draft standard that defines how such a request and response are to be made. Though useful for networks in which nodes may be connected through virtual circuits, it has far less application to Ethernet networks.

DRARP (RFC 1931)

RFC 1931, "Dynamic RARP Extensions for Automatic Network Address Acquisition," is an informational document that describes a version of RARP that includes extensions to make it more useful as a configuration protocol. The DRARP protocol was implemented on Sun Microsystems systems in the late 1980s, but its functionality has been superseded by the Dynamic Host Configuration Protocol (DHCP) described in draft standard RFC 2131. Basically, DRARP allowed the RARP server to associate IP addresses dynamically with the MAC addresses it maintained, acting as a configuration server for diskless workstations. It is mentioned here for completeness' sake more than for its relevance.

Directed ARP (RFC 1433)

Some link layer networks, such as ATM and SMDS, can span more than one IP network. In these cases, two nodes connected to the same link layer network but different IP networks will have trouble making a direct connection. They can not use a shortcut across the IP networks even though they are connected to the same link layer network. One experimental approach to solving this problem (a problem because it causes routing and switching inefficiencies) is described in RFC 1433, "Directed ARP." According to the RFC, "Directed ARP is a dynamic address resolution procedure that enables hosts and routers to resolve advertised potential next-hop IP addresses on foreign IP networks to their associated link level addresses."

Again, DARP is mentioned here for completeness' sake rather than for its relevance to Ethernet. Better approaches to this problem have been developed, notably the Next Hop Resolution Protocol (NHRP) described in RFC 2332 and RFC 2333 (see also *Essential ATM Standards: RFCs and Protocols Made Practical*, Wiley 1999).

NBMA and ATM ARP

Although it was defined with a broadcast medium like Ethernet in mind, ARP has been successfully applied to nonbroadcast network technologies. RFC 1735, "NBMA Address Resolution Protocol," describes an experimental protocol for doing ARP over nonbroadcast multiple access (NBMA) networks, such as ATM and Frame Relay. Proposed standard RFC 2225, "Classical IP and ARP over ATM," provides another refinement. These versions of ARP generally rely on a server to act on behalf of attached clients, who must all register as they enter the network. For more about these protocols see *Essential ATM Standards: RFCs and Protocols Made Practical* (Wiley 1999).

Reading List

Table 10.3 contains a list of the RFCs mentioned in this chapter.

Table 10.3 RFCs Related to Address Resolution

RFC	STATUS	TITLE
RFC 826	STD 37	An Ethernet Address Resolution Protocol—or—Converting Network Protocol Addresses to 48.bit Ethernet Address for Transmission on Ethernet Hardware
RFC 903	STD 38	Reverse Address Resolution Protocol
RFC 1433	Experimental	Directed ARP
RFC 1735	Experimental	NBMA Address Resolution Protocol
RFC 1931	Informational	Dynamic RARP Extensions for Automatic Network Address Acquisition
RFC 2002	Proposed Standard	IP Mobility Support
RFC 2225	Proposed Standard	Classical IP and ARP over ATM
RFC 2390	Draft Standard	Inverse Address Resolution Protocol

CHAPTER 11

Internet Protocol Version 4 over Ethernet

In this chapter, we discuss Internet standards for the standard for transmitting IP over experimental Ethernet (STD 42, RFC 895), for transmitting IP over (nonexperimental) Ethernet (STD 41, RFC 894), and for transmitting IP over IEEE 802 networks (STD 43, RFC 1042). Unlike many other Internet standards, these specifications are relatively straightforward and concise: RFC 894 and RFC 895 are each only two and a half pages long, and RFC 1042 is only 15 pages (of which more than five pages are specific to token ring and token bus networks).

The basic issues related to running IP over any link layer protocol are as follows:

Framing. How does the IP packet get encapsulated within the link layer protocol data unit?

Address mapping. How are IP addresses to be mapped to local link network addresses?

Maximum transmission unit size. How big an IP packet can the local link carry without requiring fragmentation?

EXPERIMENTAL ETHERNET AND RFC 895

Experimental Ethernet refers to the original version of Ethernet described by Metcalfe and Boggs in their 1976 CACM paper. This was 3Mbps and used 8-bit addresses. Though RFC 895, "A Standard for the Transmission of IP Datagrams over Experimental Ethernet Networks," is also a standard (STD 42), you are not likely to see too many experimental Ethernet networks in use today. The biggest difference between STD 42 and STD 41 is that the 8-bit link layer address is easily mapped onto the last octet of a node's IP address, thus obviating the need for any kind of address resolution mechanism.

In this chapter, we discuss each of these issues, as well as the issue of interoperability between Ethernet and IEEE 802.3 networks. Issues of broadcast and multicast, also very important for any discussion of link layer protocols, are reserved for Chapter 13. We start with RFC 1122 (STD 3), "Requirements for Internet Hosts—Communication Layers," to see what it says about supporting Ethernet and IEEE 802.3.

Host and Router Requirements

In RFC 1122, "Requirements for Internet Hosts—Communication Layers," requirements for IP nodes attached to Ethernet/IEEE 802.3 networks (and networks in general) are laid out. RFC 1812, "Requirements for IP Version 4 Routers," is a proposed standard that specifies requirements for routers attached to local links as well. Routers, as a special type of host, must conform to the host requirements as well as the router specification.

Host Requirements

RFC 894 is specified as defining the standard for IP encapsulation in Ethernet networks, and RFC 1042 is specified as defining the standard for IP encapsulation in IEEE 802 networks. What RFC 1122 adds is the following set of specifications for behaviors by Internet hosts connected to a 10Mbps Ethernet cable (from RFC 1122 section 2.3.3):

- MUST be able to send and receive packets using RFC-894 encapsulation

- SHOULD be able to receive RFC-1042 packets, intermixed with RFC-894 packets

- MAY be able to send packets using RFC-1042 encapsulation

In other words, the fundamental standard remains Ethernet, though standards-compliant devices can be expected to accept IEEE 802.3 as well as Ethernet frames from the same network interface. This combination ensures that implementations that support IEEE 802.3 are not put at a disadvantage in terms of deployment in networks where Ethernet is usually used (since all hosts must be able to receive IEEE 802.3 frames), but that support for IEEE 802.3 is not (and is not likely to become) a requirement.

> **NOTE** RFC 2119 (BCP 14), "Key Words for Use in RFCs to Indicate Requirement Levels," defines the keyword SHOULD to mean that "there may exist valid reasons in particular circumstances to ignore a particular item, but the full implications must be understood and carefully weighed before choosing a different course." The word MAY means that "an item is truly optional. One vendor may choose to include the item because a particular marketplace requires it or because the vendor feels that it enhances the product while another vendor may omit the same item. An implementation that does not include a particular option MUST be prepared to interoperate with another implementation that does include the option, though perhaps with reduced functionality. In the same vein, an implementation that does include a particular option MUST be prepared to interoperate with another implementation that does not include the option (except, of course, for the feature the option provides.)"

LLC and SNAP

RFC 1122 notes that although the IEEE reserved the Service Access Point (SAP) value of 6 to be used in the LLC header (see Chapter 8) to specify IP in the payload, this value should not be used. LLC by itself does not allow the use of EtherType in the link layer headers. When carrying IP the SNAP header is necessary, so the SAP values (DSAP and SSAP) must be set to 170 to indicate that SNAP headers follow the LLC headers. Internet standard systems must not use SAP values of 6, but rather values of 170.

Address Resolution and Maximum Transmission Unit

RFC 1122 specifies that the Address Resolution Protocol (ARP) must be used for both Ethernet and for all IEEE 802 network link layer address translations. ARP (RFC 826, STD 37) was discussed in Chapter 10. Although static translation tables are possible, they are not permitted by the standard.

The Maximum Transmission Unit (MTU) is specified as 1500 bytes for Ethernet and 1492 for IEEE 802.3 networks. Ethernet supports a maximum frame size of 1518 bytes: 6 bytes each for source and destination MAC addresses (12) plus 2 bytes for the EtherType/frame length field (14) plus 1500 bytes for the payload (1514) plus 4 bytes for the frame check sequence field (1518).

Ethernet encapsulation allows as much as 1500 byte payloads made up entirely of higher-layer protocol data, while IEEE 802.3 adds 8 bytes of additional overhead for IP payloads: the LLC headers (3 bytes) plus the SNAP headers (5 bytes). Thus, IEEE 802.3 payloads can carry only 1492 of IP datagram per frame.

Mixing Ethernet and IEEE 802.3

Ethernet and IEEE 802.3 frames are easily distinguished. Just check the EtherType/frame length field. If its value is in the range of 46 through 1500 (inclusive), then it is an IEEE 802.3 frame. If it is 1501 or higher, it is an Ethernet frame.

Compatibility between the two is possible only if all nodes support receiving both Ethernet and IEEE 802.3 frames. Given RFC 1122's specification that all IP hosts should do this, interoperability is largely ensured. RFC 1122 also notes that where nodes are able to receive only one type of frame, broadcasts in one framing type can be received only by nodes supporting that framing type. In a hypothetical network containing Ethernet-only nodes and IEEE 802.3-only nodes, broadcasts from Ethernet nodes would reach only other Ethernet nodes and broadcasts from IEEE 802.3 nodes would reach only other Ethernet nodes.

One solution to this problem would be to assign the Ethernet nodes on a single link to one IP subnet and all IEEE 802.3 nodes on that link to a different subnet. The different nodes would thus be able to communicate through a router, but not directly via layer 2.

Router Requirements

RFC 1812, "Requirements for IP Version 4 Routers," specifies how routers should behave. This RFC repeatedly cites RFC 1122 ("Requirements for Internet Hosts - Communication Layers") which is part of STD-3. Because a router is also a host, it must conform to the Internet hosts requirements. Beyond that, there is little more to say about requirements for routers connecting to Ethernet networks: They must simply behave as any Ethernet host as well as behave as any other type of router.

IP Datagrams over Ethernet Networks

RFC 894 (STD 41), "A Standard for the Transmission of IP Datagrams over Ethernet Networks," was published in April 1984 and written by Charles Hornig of the Symbolics Cambridge Research Center. It is about two and a half pages long, including header, introduction, and references. It is clear and to the point in explaining how IP is to be transmitted over 10Mbps Ethernets. The relevant sections are reproduced here, with references included at the end of this section. RFC 894 should be considered in the context both of host and router requirements discussed in the previous section, but also in the context of the standard for transmitting IP packets over IEEE 802 networks, discussed in the section following this one.

This document discusses the use of trailer encapsulations and references the informational RFC 893, "Trailer Encapsulations." The argument for trailer encapsulations, in which the data of a frame is put first and the headers are put last ("trailing") to take advantage of efficiencies related to memory copying functions in some versions of Unix 4.2bsd. This type of encapsulation is permitted only when the source knows that the destination node will accept it. Nodes may query each other at the link layer to determine if this type of encapsulation is desirable, but it may not be used as a default encapsulation.

The rest of this section is printed in the Courier font to indicate that it is quoted directly from RFC 894.

Frame Format

```
IP datagrams are transmitted in standard Ethernet frames.  The type
field of the Ethernet frame must contain the value hexadecimal 0800.
The data field contains the IP header followed immediately by the IP
data.

The minimum length of the data field of a packet sent over an
Ethernet is 46 octets.  If necessary, the data field should be padded
(with octets of zero) to meet the Ethernet minimum frame size.  This
padding is not part of the IP packet and is not included in the total
length field of the IP header.

The minimum length of the data field of a packet sent over an
Ethernet is 1500 octets, thus the maximum length of an IP datagram
sent over an Ethernet is 1500 octets.  Implementations are encouraged
to support full-length packets.  Gateway implementations MUST be
prepared to accept full-length packets and fragment them if
necessary.  If a system cannot receive full-length packets, it should
```

take steps to discourage others from sending them, such as using the TCP Maximum Segment Size option [4].

NOTE

Datagrams on the Ethernet may be longer than the general Internet default maximum packet size of 576 octets. Hosts connected to an Ethernet should keep this in mind when sending datagrams to hosts not on the same Ethernet. It may be appropriate to send smaller datagrams to avoid unnecessary fragmentation at intermediate gateways. Please see [4] for further information on this point.

Address Mappings

The mapping of 32-bit Internet addresses to 48-bit Ethernet addresses can be done several ways. A static table could be used, or a dynamic discovery procedure could be used.

Static Table

Each host could be provided with a table of all other hosts on the local network with both their Ethernet and Internet addresses.

Dynamic Discovery

Mappings between 32-bit Internet addresses and 48-bit Ethernet addresses could be accomplished through the Address Resolution Protocol (ARP) [5]. Internet addresses are assigned arbitrarily on some Internet network. Each host's implementation must know its own Internet address and respond to Ethernet Address Resolution packets appropriately. It should also use ARP to translate Internet addresses to Ethernet addresses when needed.

Broadcast Address

The broadcast Internet address (the address on that network with a host part of all binary ones) should be mapped to the broadcast Ethernet address (of all binary ones, FF-FF-FF-FF-FF-FF hex).

The use of the ARP dynamic discovery procedure is strongly recommended.

Trailer Formats

Some versions of Unix 4.2bsd use a different encapsulation method in order to get better network performance with the VAX virtual memory architecture. Consenting systems on the same Ethernet may use this format between themselves.

No host is required to implement it, and no datagrams in this format should be sent to any host unless the sender has positive knowledge that the recipient will be able to interpret them. Details of the trailer encapsulation may be found in [6].

(Note: At the present time Unix 4.2bsd will either always use trailers or never use them (per interface), depending on a boot-time option. This is expected to be changed in the future. Unix 4.2bsd also uses a non-standard Internet broadcast address with a host part of all zeroes, this may also be changed in the future.)

Byte Order

As described in Appendix B of the Internet Protocol specification [1], the IP datagram is transmitted over the Ethernet as a series of 8-bit bytes.

References

[1] Postel, J., "Internet Protocol", RFC-791, USC/Information Sciences Institute, September 1981.

[2] "The Ethernet - A Local Area Network", Version 1.0, Digital Equipment Corporation, Intel Corporation, Xerox Corporation, September 1980.

[3] Postel, J., "A Standard for the Transmission of IP Datagrams over Experimental Ethernet Networks", RFC-895, USC/Information Sciences Institute, April 1984.

[4] Postel, J., "The TCP Maximum Segment Size Option and Related Topics", RFC-879, USC/Information Sciences Institute, November 1983.

[5] Plummer, D., "An Ethernet Address Resolution Protocol", RFC-826, Symbolics Cambridge Research Center, November 1982.

[6] Leffler, S., and M. Karels, "Trailer Encapsulations", RFC-893, University of California at Berkeley, April 1984.

IP Datagrams over IEEE 802 Networks

RFC 1042 (STD 43), "A Standard for the Transmission of IP Datagrams over IEEE 802 Networks," defines a standard method for encapsulating IP packets (and ARP packets) on IEEE 802 networks of all types, including IEEE 802.3 (Ethernet), IEEE 802.4 (token bus), and IEEE 802.5 (token ring).

It makes sense to excerpt the relevant portions of this RFC as we did in the last section. J. Postel and J. Reynolds wrote RFC 1042, published in February 1988. As before, text that appears in Courier font is taken directly from the RFC. The memo status and acknowledgment sections have not been included, nor have sections discussing token bus and token ring networks. References are included at the end of this section.

Introduction

```
The goal of this specification is to allow compatible and
interoperable implementations for transmitting IP datagrams and ARP
requests and replies.  To achieve this it may be necessary in a few
cases to limit the use that IP and ARP make of the capabilities of a
particular IEEE 802 standard.

The IEEE 802 specifications define a family of standards for Local
Area Networks (LANs) that deal with the Physical and Data Link Layers
as defined by the ISO Open System Interconnection Reference Model
(ISO/OSI).  Several Physical Layer standards (802.3, 802.4, and
802.5) [3,4,5] and one Data Link Layer Standard (802.2) [6] have been
defined.  The IEEE Physical Layer standards specify the ISO/OSI
Physical Layer and the Media Access Control Sublayer of the ISO/OSI
Data Link Layer.  The 802.2 Data Link Layer standard specifies the
Logical Link Control Sublayer of the ISO/OSI Data Link Layer.

This memo describes the use of IP and ARP on the three types of
networks.  At this time, it is not necessary that the use of IP and
ARP be consistent across all three types of networks, only that it be
consistent within each type.  This may change in the future as new
IEEE 802 standards are defined and the existing standards are revised
allowing for interoperability at the Data Link Layer.

It is the goal of this memo to specify enough about the use of IP and
ARP on each type of network to ensure that:

        (1) all equipment using IP or ARP on 802.3 networks will
        interoperate,

        (2) all equipment using IP or ARP on 802.4 networks will
        interoperate,

        (3) all equipment using IP or ARP on 802.5 networks will
        interoperate.

Of course, the goal of IP is interoperability between computers
attached to different networks, when those networks are
interconnected via an IP gateway [8].  The use of IEEE 802.1
compatible Transparent Bridges to allow interoperability across
different networks is not fully described pending completion of that
standard.
```

Description

IEEE 802 networks may be used as IP networks of any class (A, B, or C). These systems use two Link Service Access Point (LSAP) fields of the LLC header in much the same way the ARPANET uses the "link" field. Further, there is an extension of the LLC header called the Sub-Network Access Protocol (SNAP).

IP datagrams are sent on IEEE 802 networks encapsulated within the 802.2 LLC and SNAP data link layers, and the 802.3, 802.4, or 802.5 physical networks layers. The SNAP is used with an Organization Code indicating that the following 16 bits specify the EtherType code (as listed in Assigned Numbers [7]).

Normally, all communication is performed using 802.2 type 1 communication. Consenting systems on the same IEEE 802 network may use 802.2 type 2 communication after verifying that it is supported by both nodes. This is accomplished using the 802.2 XID mechanism. However, type 1 communication is the recommended method at this time and must be supported by all implementations. The rest of this specification assumes the use of type 1 communication.

The IEEE 802 networks may have 16-bit or 48-bit physical addresses. This specification allows the use of either size of address within a given IEEE 802 network.

Note that the 802.3 standard specifies a transmission rate of from 1 to 20 megabit/second, the 802.4 standard specifies 1, 5, and 10 megabit/second, and the 802.5 standard specifies 1 and 4 megabit/second. The typical transmission rates used are 10 megabit/second for 802.3, 10 megabit/second for 802.4, and 4 megabit/second for 802.5. However, this specification for the transmission of IP Datagrams does not depend on the transmission rate.

Header Format

```
                                                          Header

...--------+--------+--------+
          MAC Header        |                   802.{3/4/5} MAC
...--------+--------+--------+


+--------+--------+--------+
| DSAP=K1| SSAP=K1| Control|                       802.2 LLC
+--------+--------+--------+


+--------+--------+--------+--------+--------+
|Protocol Id or Org Code =K2|   EtherType    |       802.2 SNAP
+--------+--------+--------+--------+--------+
```

The total length of the LLC Header and the SNAP header is 8-octets, making the 802.2 protocol overhead come out on an nice boundary.

The K1 value is 170 (decimal).

The K2 value is 0 (zero).

The control value is 3 (Unnumbered Information).

Address Mappings

The mapping of 32-bit Internet addresses to 16-bit or 48-bit IEEE 802 addresses must be done via the dynamic discovery procedure of the Address Resolution Protocol (ARP) [2].

Internet addresses are assigned arbitrarily on Internet networks. Each host's implementation must know its own Internet address and respond to Address Resolution requests appropriately. It must also use ARP to translate Internet addresses to IEEE 802 addresses when needed.

The ARP Details

The ARP protocol has several fields that parameterize its use in any specific context [2]. These fields are:

```
    hrd     16 - bits       The Hardware Type Code
    pro     16 - bits       The Protocol Type Code
    hln      8 - bits       Octets in each hardware address
    pln      8 - bits       Octets in each protocol address
    op      16 - bits       Operation Code
```

The hardware type code assigned for the IEEE 802 networks (of all kinds) is 6 (see [7] page 16).

The protocol type code for IP is 2048 (see [7] page 14).

The hardware address length is 2 for 16-bit IEEE 802 addresses, or 6 for 48-bit IEEE 802 addresses.

The protocol address length (for IP) is 4.

The operation code is 1 for request and 2 for reply.

Broadcast Address

The broadcast Internet address (the address on that network with a host part of all binary ones) should be mapped to the broadcast IEEE 802 address (of all binary ones) (see [8] page 14).

Trailer Formats

Some versions of Unix 4.x bsd use a different encapsulation method in order to get better network performance with the VAX virtual memory architecture. Consenting systems on the same IEEE 802 network may use this format between themselves. Details of the trailer encapsulation method may be found in [9]. However, all hosts must be able to communicate using the standard (non-trailer) method.

Byte Order

As described in Appendix B of the Internet Protocol specification [1], the IP datagram is transmitted over IEEE 802 networks as a series of 8-bit bytes. This byte transmission order has been called "big-endian" [11].

Maximum Transmission Unit

The Maximum Transmission Unit (MTU) differs on the different types of IEEE 802 networks. In the following there are comments on the MTU for each type of IEEE 802 network. However, on any particular network all hosts must use the same MTU. In the following, the terms "maximum packet size" and "maximum transmission unit" are equivalent.

Frame Format and MAC Level Issues

For all hardware types

IP datagrams and ARP requests and replies are transmitted in standard 802.2 LLC Type 1 Unnumbered Information format, control code 3, with the DSAP and the SSAP fields of the 802.2 header set to 170, the assigned global SAP value for SNAP [6]. The 24-bit Organization Code in the SNAP is zero, and the remaining 16 bits are the EtherType from Assigned Numbers [7] (IP = 2048, ARP = 2054).

IEEE 802 packets may have a minimum size restriction. When necessary, the data field should be padded (with octets of zero) to meet the IEEE 802 minimum frame size requirements. This padding is not part of the IP datagram and is not included in the total length field of the IP header.

For compatibility (and common sense) the minimum packet size used with IP datagrams is 28 octets, which is 20 (minimum IP header) + 8 (LLC+SNAP header) = 28 octets (not including the MAC header).

The minimum packet size used with ARP is 24 octets, which is 20 (ARP with 2 octet hardware addresses and 4 octet protocol addresses) + 8 (LLC+SNAP header) = 24 octets (not including the

MAC header).

In typical situations, the packet size used with ARP is 32 octets, which is 28 (ARP with 6 octet hardware addresses and 4 octet protocol addresses) + 8 (LLC+SNAP header) = 32 octets (not including the MAC header).

IEEE 802 packets may have a maximum size restriction. Implementations are encouraged to support full-length packets.

For compatibility purposes, the maximum packet size used with IP datagrams or ARP requests and replies must be consistent on a particular network.

Gateway implementations must be prepared to accept full-length packets and fragment them when necessary.

Host implementations should be prepared to accept full-length packets, however hosts must not send datagrams longer than 576 octets unless they have explicit knowledge that the destination is prepared to accept them. A host may communicate its size preference in TCP based applications via the TCP Maximum Segment Size option [10].

Datagrams on IEEE 802 networks may be longer than the general Internet default maximum packet size of 576 octets. Hosts connected to an IEEE 802 network should keep this in mind when sending datagrams to hosts not on the same IEEE 802 network. It may be appropriate to send smaller datagrams to avoid unnecessary fragmentation at intermediate gateways. Please see [10] for further information.

IEEE 802.2 Details

While not necessary for supporting IP and ARP, all implementations are required to support IEEE 802.2 standard Class I service. This requires supporting Unnumbered Information (UI) Commands, eXchange IDentification (XID) Commands and Responses, and TEST link (TEST) Commands and Responses.

When either an XID or a TEST command is received a response must be returned; with the Destination and Source addresses, and the DSAP and SSAP swapped.

When responding to an XID or a TEST command the sense of the poll/final bit must be preserved. That is, a command received with the poll/final bit reset must have the response returned with the poll/final bit reset and vice versa.

The XID command or response has an LLC control field value of 175 (decimal) if poll is off or 191 (decimal) if poll is on. (See Appendix on Numbers.)

The TEST command or response has an LLC control field value of 227 (decimal) if poll is off or 243 (decimal) if poll is on. (See Appendix on Numbers.)

A command frame is identified with high order bit of the SSAP address reset. Response frames have high order bit of the SSAP address set to one.

XID response frames should include an 802.2 XID Information field of 129.1.0 indicating Class I (connectionless) service. (type 1).

TEST response frames should echo the information field received in the corresponding TEST command frame.

For IEEE 802.3

A particular implementation of an IEEE 802.3 Physical Layer is denoted using a three field notation. The three fields are data rate in megabit/second, medium type, and maximum segment length in hundreds of meters. One combination of of 802.3 parameters is 10BASE5 which specifies a 10 megabit/second transmission rate, baseband medium, and 500 meter segments. This correspondes to the specifications of the familiar "ethernet" network.

The MAC header contains 6 (2) octets of source address, 6 (2) octets of destination address, and 2 octets of length. The MAC trailer contains 4 octets of Frame Check Sequence (FCS), for a total of 18 (10) octets.

IEEE 802.3 networks have a minimum packet size that depends on the transmission rate. For type 10BASE5 802.3 networks the minimum packet size is 64 octets.

IEEE 802.3 networks have a maximum packet size which depends on the transmission rate. For type 10BASE5 802.3 networks the maximum packet size is 1518 octets including all octets between the destination address and the FCS inclusive.

This allows 1518 - 18 (MAC header+trailer) - 8 (LLC+SNAP header) = 1492 for the IP datagram (including the IP header). Note that 1492 is not equal to 1500 which is the MTU for ethernet networks.

[discussions of IEEE 802.4 and 802.5 deleted]

Interoperation with Ethernet

It is possible to use the ethernet link level protocol [12] on the same physical cable with the IEEE 802.3 link level protocol. A computer interfaced to a physical cable used in this way could potentially read both ethernet and 802.3 packets from the network. If a computer does read both types of packets, it must keep track of which link protocol was used with each other computer on the network and use the proper link protocol when sending packets.

One should note that in such an environment, link level broadcast packets will not reach all the computers attached to the network, but only those using the link level protocol used for the broadcast.

Since it must be assumed that most computers will read and send using only one type of link protocol, it is recommended that if such an environment (a network with both link protocols) is necessary, an IP gateway be used as if there were two distinct networks.

Note that the MTU for the Ethernet allows a 1500 octet IP datagram, with the MTU for the 802.3 network allows only a 1492 octet IP datagram.

Appendix on Numbers

The IEEE likes to specify numbers in bit transmission order, or bit-wise little-endian order. The Internet protocols are documented in byte-wise big-endian order. This may cause some confusion about the proper values to use for numbers. Here are the conversions for some numbers of interest.

Number	IEEE HEX	IEEE Binary	Internet Binary	Internet Decimal
UI Op Code	C0	11000000	00000011	3
SAP for SNAP	55	01010101	10101010	170
XID	F5	11110101	10101111	175
XID	FD	11111101	10111111	191
TEST	C7	11000111	11100011	227
TEST	CF	11001111	11110011	243
Info	818000			129.1.0

References

[1]   Postel, J., "Internet Protocol", RFC-791, USC/Information Sciences Institute, September 1981.

[2]   Plummer, D., "An Ethernet Address Resolution Protocol - or - Converting Network Protocol Addresses to 48.bit Ethernet

Address for Transmission on Ethernet Hardware", RFC-826, MIT, November 1982.

[3]   IEEE, "IEEE Standards for Local Area Networks: Carrier Sense Multiple Access with Collision Detection (CSMA/CD) Access Method and Physical Layer Specifications", IEEE, New York, New York, 1985.

[4]   IEEE, "IEEE Standards for Local Area Networks: Token-Passing Bus Access Method and Physical Layer Specification", IEEE, New York, New York, 1985.

[5]   IEEE, "IEEE Standards for Local Area Networks: Token Ring Access Method and Physical Layer Specifications", IEEE, New York, New York, 1985.

[6]   IEEE, "IEEE Standards for Local Area Networks: Logical Link Control", IEEE, New York, New York, 1985.

[7]   Reynolds, J.K., and J. Postel, "Assigned Numbers", RFC-1010, USC/Information Sciences Institute, May 1987.

[8]   Braden, R., and J. Postel, "Requirements for Internet Gateways", RFC-1009, USC/Information Sciences Institute, June 1987.

[9]   Leffler, S., and M. Karels, "Trailer Encapsulations", RFC-893, University of California at Berkeley, April 1984.

[10] Postel, J., "The TCP Maximum Segment Size Option and Related Topics", RFC-879, USC/Information Sciences Institute, November 1983.

[11] Cohen, D., "On Holy Wars and a Plea for Peace", Computer, IEEE, October 1981.

[12] D-I-X, "The Ethernet - A Local Area Network: Data Link Layer and Physical Layer Specifications", Digital, Intel, and Xerox, November 1982.

[13] IBM, "Token-Ring Network Architecture Reference", Second Edition, SC30-3374-01, August 1987.

Path MTU Discovery

RFC 1191, "Path MTU Discovery," defines a draft standard for determining the maximum transmission unit over all the networks that an IP packet traverses between a source and destination node. Path MTU discovery takes advantage of the Don't Fragment bit in the IP header (see RFC 791, "Internet Protocol") to determine how big a packet can be sent over a particular route at a particular time. When a packet is transmitted that is too large to make it through an intermediate link without fragmentation, the router notes that the Don't Fragment has been set and sends back an ICMP Destination Unreachable message that includes the MTU of the next link. The source node then resends a smaller packet, which should be able to pass through that link.

As the packet continues on its way, it may encounter another link with a smaller MTU. In this case, the process is repeated. RFC 1191 lists several different link layer types commonly used up to that time (1990), along with their associated MTUs. Though most still have some significance (see Table 11.1), the most important are Ethernet, IEEE 802.3, and PPP. ATM is not even listed, as it was not around back then.

Table 11.1 Common MTUs Found on the Internet in 1990 (from RFC 1191)

NETWORK/COMMENTS	MTU (OCTETS)	RFC REFERENCE
Official Maximum for IPv4	65535	RFC 791
Hyperchannel	65535	RFC 1044
IBM Token Ring	17914	RFC 1191
IEEE 802.4	8166	RFC 1042
IEEE 802.5 (4Mbps Token Ring, maximum MTU)	4464	RFC 1042
FDDI	4352	RFC 1188
Wideband Network	2048	RFC 907
IEEE 802.5 (4Mbps Token Ring, recommended MTU)	2002	RFC 1042
Experimental Ethernet	1536	RFC 895
Ethernet	1500	RFC 894
Point-to-Point Protocol (PPP)	1500	RFC 1134
IEEE 802.3	1492	RFC 1042
SLIP	1006	RFC 1055
X.25	576	RFC 877
NetBIOS	512	RFC 1088
Official Minimum MTU	68	RFC 791

Reading List

The RFCs mentioned in this chapter are listed in Table 11.2.

Table 11.2 RFCs Covering IP Over Ethernet and IEEE 802 Networks

RFC	STATUS	TITLE
RFC 791	STD 5	Internet Protocol
RFC 826	STD 37	An Ethernet Address Resolution Protocol—or—Converting Network Protocol Addresses to 48.bit Ethernet Address for Transmission on Ethernet Hardware
RFC 893	Informational	Trailer Encapsulations
RFC 894	STD 41	Standard for the Transmission of IP Datagrams over Ethernet Networks (IP-E)
RFC 895	STD 42	Standard for the Transmission of IP Datagrams over Experimental Ethernet Networks (IP-EE)
RFC 1042	STD 43	Standard for the Transmission of IP Datagrams over IEEE 802 Networks
RFC 1122	STD 3	Requirements for Internet Hosts—Communication Layers
RFC 1191	Draft Standard	Path MTU Discovery
RFC 1812	Proposed Standard	Requirements for IP Version 4 Routers

Internet Protocol Version 6 over Ethernet

A next-generation version of the Internet Protocol was first foreseen as a necessity in the early 1990s when it became apparent that the 32-bit address space defined for IPv4 was being rapidly allocated and would soon be exhausted. That revision to IP, IP version 6 (IPv6) was initially specified in published RFCs in late 1995 (RFC 1883, "Internet Protocol, Version 6 (IPv6) Specification") and has since been updated and published with the same title as a draft standard in RFC 2460, in 1999.

In addition to defining a 128-bit address space, which should be sufficiently large to accommodate as many nodes and networks as can be reasonably foreseen, IPv6 incorporates a number of updates and enhancements to the basic Internet Protocol used since the late 1970s and early 1980s. One of these changes is the elimination of broadcasts; another is the replacement of the Address Resolution Protocol (ARP) by a new mechanism for transmitting packets across a local link: neighbor discovery. Another change is the use of a global network identifier, based on IEEE standard EUI-64, for configuring IPv6 node addresses. Stateless autoconfiguration is an enhancement added to IPv6 to allow for plug-and-play connectivity to IPv6 networks: Nodes can plug into the network and achieve connectivity without any prearrangement with network administrators and without the user having to know or do anything special. Each of these developments has implications for the way IPv6 operates over Ethernet.

A full discussion of IPv6 is beyond the scope of this chapter (for more information about IPv6, see the author's *IPv6 Clearly Explained*, Morgan Kaufmann, 1999). However, we first discuss the IPv6 addressing architecture defined in RFC 2373, "IP Version 6 Addressing Architecture," and the use of EUI-64 network addressing. Next, we outline the neighbor discovery protocol as defined in RFC 2461, "Neighbor Discovery for IP Version 6." This is followed by an overview of the stateless autoconfiguration protocol defined in RFC 2462, "IPv6 Stateless Address Autoconfiguration." Finally, we look at the actual mechanics of running IPv6 over Ethernet as defined by RFC 2464, "Transmission of IPv6 Packets over Ethernet Networks."

IPv6 Addressing Architecture

IPv6 actually attempts to solve two separate problems with IPv4. The most obvious problem arises from IPv4's 32-bit address space. Even if it were not allocated into an inefficient class structure, a 32-bit address space can support no more than about four billion unique addresses if it could be used with 100 percent efficiency. As it is, IPv4 is limited to somewhat more than 2 million routable network addresses. With millions of businesses around the world seeking Internet connectivity, workarounds and stopgap measures have been used to prevent problems.

This is the root of the other problem that IPv6 solves: the spiraling growth of the Internet routing tables. Each separate network needs to have a separate routing table entry in the Internet backbone routers. Classless Inter-Domain Routing (CIDR), published in 1993 as a proposed standard in RFC 1519, "Classless Inter-Domain Routing (CIDR): An Address Assignment and Aggregation Strategy," allows many routes to be collapsed into a single route through the use of aggregation. However, routing tables are still out of hand in many cases, and a more highly aggregatable approach is needed to prevent routing table meltdown.

In this section we take a quick look at the IPv6 address space, IPv6 address aggregation, and the IEEE EUI-64 standard for link layer addressing.

IPv6 Aggregatable Addresses

IPv6 addresses are 128 bits long. The high-order n bits represent the network address, and the low-order 128-n bits represent the interface address. Figure 12.1 shows a format for IPv6 addresses, as defined in RFC 2373. This is a very generalized version of the IPv6 address: It shows little more than that the high-order bits represent a network and the low-order bits represent the interface on the local link. Of course, this is quite vague, but it demonstrates a basic tenet of IPv6 aggregatable addressing—that forwarding decisions are to be made based on the "longest prefix match" algorithm. In other words, routers make decisions about routing packets by matching the destination address network prefix against a routing table. All nodes on the same link share the same network prefix, and the longest possible match (in this case) is n bits.

The format shown in Figure 12.1 is overly general, but Figure 12.2 provides a clearer view of how IPv6 aggregatable addressing works. Taken from RFC 2374, it demonstrates several characteristics of IPv6 addresses. First, n = 64: the network portion of the address is 64 bits long, and the interface ID portion of the address is also 64 bits long. This provides plenty of addressing space both for individual networks. Every subnet can support as many as $2^{64} - 1$ or about 18 million trillion nodes. Roughly the same number of networks can supported by the IPv6 address space (although only a small portion of the address space has been allocated to be used for aggregatable addresses so far).

It also demonstrates that the network address space (the high-order 64 bits) is highly structured to support aggregated routing tables. At the extreme left, the first three bits contain a format prefix that identifies the type of IPv6 address; aggregatable global unicast addresses are represented by 001. Other types of addresses have been reserved, but the focus is on aggregatable addresses so far.

The next 61 bits are used for three layers of aggregation: top-level, next-level, and site-level aggregation. Top-level aggregation identifies as

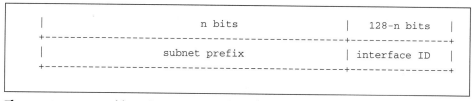

Figure 12.1   IPv6 address format (from RFC 2373).

```
                 | 3|  13 | 8 |    24    |   16   |            64 bits
|

    +--+-----+---+--------+--------+-----------------------------------+
    |FP| TLA |RES| NLA    | SLA    |            Interface ID           |
    |  | ID  |   | ID     | ID     |                                   |
    +--+-----+---+--------+--------+-----------------------------------+

    <--Public Topology--->   Site
                           <-------->
                           Topology
                                    <------Interface Identifier----->

  Where

      FP              Format Prefix (001)
      TLA ID          Top-Level Aggregation Identifier
      RES             Reserved for future use
      NLA ID          Next-Level Aggregation Identifier
      SLA ID          Site-Level Aggregation Identifier
      INTERFACE ID    Interface Identifier
```

Figure 12.2   IPv6 aggregatable address format (from RFC 2374).

many as 8192 (2^{13}) entities that maintain responsibility for routing huge amounts of the IPv6 address space. So far, there are no top-level entities assigned, but they would likely be large telecommunications firms with hundreds of millions of subscribers, or perhaps even countries. Such an entity would be assigned a 16-bit prefix and would be able to allocate network addresses with that prefix as it wishes. A global ISP with a top-level address (TLA) would distribute some site next-level addresses (NLAs) to the ISPs who buy service from the TLA ISP. It could also resell site-level addresses (SLAs) to its own end-user customers.

Routing aggregation works like this: A router receives a packet and checks the destination address. If the packet is destined for a node in the same TLA as the router (the first 16 bits are the same as the router's address), the router checks further in its routing table for a longer match. If there is no longer match, the router passes the packet to another router (which is likely to be a backbone router) within that TLA. If there is a longer match, it means the destination shares the NLA address with the destination, which means that a local or regional ISP may handle services for the networks of both the source and destination nodes. If the destination address prefix matches a prefix for a site-level aggregation identifier, the source and destination are in the same organizational entity.

This approach ensures that routing tables remain relatively small. A router will have more complexity regarding routes to "close" destinations, while "far" destinations will be aggregated into an "over-there" route.

When talking about running IPv6 over Ethernet, what is of greatest interest to us is not so much the way the network addresses are allocated and aggregated, but the way the interface IDs are assigned. In IPv4, interface addresses, or host addresses, are either assigned and administered manually or are dynamically assigned through the Dynamic Host Configuration Service (DHCP). In any case, the host IP addresses tend to be in short supply due to the way IPv4 addresses are structured. In Class C addresses, which are most plentiful and quite common, the fourth octet of the IP address is devoted to the interface address. This means that no more than 254 nodes (the all-zeros and all-ones addresses are reserved) can be allocated to any Class C address. With many Class C addresses severely subnetted to support multiple sites or customers, even fewer interface addresses are available.

With 64-bit addresses, IPv6 eliminates the scarcity of interface addresses and removes the need for sharing IP addresses among nodes using DHCP. For example, ISPs often use DHCP to assign temporary IP addresses to customers using dialup services. In fact, a 64-bit interface address makes it possible for every node to take on its own globally unique address. This has important ramifications as we discuss neighbor discovery and auto-configuration, but first, we need to understand how the interface identifier is created for an IPv6 node.

IPv6 and EUI-64 Addressing

The IEEE defines standards for link layer network addressing; the 6-byte addresses common to Ethernet and other IEEE 802 network types are defined by the IEEE. More recently, an 8-byte address standard, EUI-64, was defined for globally identifying network interfaces. Whether 6 bytes long (EUI-48) or 8 bytes long (EUI-64), this is the address that is usually hard-coded into the network interface hardware. In either case, the first three (high-order) octets of the address are allocated to vendors to identify the manufacturer of the interface device; the last three (EUI-48) or five (EUI-64) octets of the address and are (supposed to be) globally unique within the vendor address space.

The seventh and eight bits of the EUI address (the last bits of the first octet of the three-octet manufacturer value) are special flag bits. The seventh bit is the universal/local bit. When it is set to 0, it means that the address was globally assigned; when set to 1 it means the address is assigned locally. The eighth bit is the individual/group bit. It indicates a unicast address when it is set to 0 and a multicast address when set to 1. In this section we consider only unicast addresses.

Because IPv6 interface addresses are 64 bits long, they contain enough space to map link layer addresses directly onto the network layer (IPv6) addresses. Because the link layer addresses are globally unique, they should be globally unique within any given IPv6 network.

This makes matters considerably simpler for doing address assignment as well as for doing address resolution, as we see in the next sections. Ethernet nodes on IPv6 networks can adapt their 48-bit addresses to make them fit into the EUI-64 format. Appendix A of RFC 2373 defines four different scenarios for creating or adapting network addresses to fit this format:

The node may have an EUI-48 address. This is the case we are most interested in. It encompasses most IEEE 802 networks and, in particular, Ethernet and IEEE 802.3 network interfaces. In this case, it is necessary to map the 48-bit address onto the 64-bit EUI-64 address format. This is done by inserting two octets (0xFF FE) in the middle of the 48-bit MAC address, dividing the vendor ID and the interface number. The universal/local bit is also toggled to indicate that the address is now a globally scoped address.

The node may already have an EUI-64 address. In this case, the address can be used almost exactly as is, except that the universal/local bit must be toggled to indicate that the address is now a globally scoped address.

The node may have a link identifier that is not globally unique. For example, LocalTalk uses an 8-bit node identifier. In this case, the node identifier is simply zero-filled to the left (the link layer identifier is placed in the low-order bits of the EUI-64 address). In this case, the universal/global bit is set to 0 (because the high-order bits are all set to zero), indicating that the address is locally scoped.

The node may have no identifier of its own, as with point-to-point links and configured tunnels. A number of approaches are possible in this case, including the use of manual configuration of an address, a random number generator, the address of a system interface that is not connected to the IPv6 network, a node serial number or some other node-specific token.

We return to the EUI-64 address later in this chapter when we cover IPv6 over Ethernet.

IPv6 Neighbor Discovery

Neighbor discovery (ND), described in draft standard RFC 2461 "Neighbor Discover for IP Version 6," relies on the use of multicast transmissions. Because of this, it is more straightforward to implement on link layer protocols that natively support multicast, such as Ethernet. However, ND is intended for use in all link types, even nonbroadcast media. Under IPv6, hosts and routers use neighbor discovery for several functions. RFC 2461 lists specific problems that ND solves. This list is quoted directly from the RFC:

Router discovery. How hosts locate routers that reside on an attached link.

Prefix discovery. How hosts discover the set of address prefixes that define which destinations are on-link for an attached link. (Nodes use prefixes to distinguish destinations that reside on-link from those only reachable through a router.)

Parameter discovery. How a node learns link parameters, such as the link MTU, or Internet parameters, such as the hop limit value, to place in outgoing packets.

Address autoconfiguration. How nodes automatically configure an address for an interface.

Address resolution. How nodes determine the link-layer address of an on-link destination (for example, a neighbor) given only the destination's IP address.

Next-hop determination. The algorithm for mapping an IP destination address into the IP address of the neighbor to which traffic for the destination should be sent. The next-hop can be a router or the destination itself.

Neighbor unreachability detection. How nodes determine that a neighbor is no longer reachable. For neighbors used as routers, alternate default routers can be tried. For both routers and hosts, address resolution can be performed again.

Duplicate address detection. How a node determines that an address it wishes to use is not already in use by another node.

Redirect. How a router informs a host of a better first-hop node to reach a particular destination.

IPv6 Multicast Addresses

Some special IPv6 multicast addresses are defined in proposed standard RFC 2373, "IP Version 6 Addressing Architecture." The general format for IPv6 multicast addresses is shown in Figure 12.3. All multicast addresses start with the hexadecimal value 0xFF. The second octet for "well-known" multicast addresses will be of the form 0x0n, where n indicates a scope. If n = 1, then the scope is the node (all group members on the node). If n = 2, the scope is widened to include the local link (all group members attached to the same local link); n = 5 widens the scope to include the "site" (the organizational or campus network). To reach all the nodes on a local link, you would use the multicast address FF02:0:0:0:0:0:0:1. The first octet is 0xFF indicating a multicast address, the second octet is 01, indicating a well-known multicast address with a link-local scope.

An important well-known multicast address type is the solicited-node multicast address. This is the address to which a node can send a request for address resolution when the node has an IPv6 address with no link layer address mapped to it. This address takes the form FF02:0:0:0:0:1:FFxx:xxxx. The last three octets (represented here as xx:xxxx) are the low-order 24 bits of the IPv6 address.

Addresses for Neighbor Discovery

Nodes (hosts and routers) use several different multicast addresses to request or receive information about routes as well as link layer addresses for neighbors. For example, the all-nodes multicast address is a link-local scoped address. (It is multicast only on the local link—it is not propagated outside the link by routers.) The all-nodes address is used by routers to send out periodic router advertisements. The solicited-node multicast address is used by nodes wishing to map a link layer address to an IPv6 address.

Neighbor discovery uses several different address types, including some multicast addresses, to fulfill all its functions. These include the following:

All-nodes link-local multicast address. This address is used to reach all nodes on the local link (FF02:0:0:0:0:0:0:1). All nodes must subscribe to this group (that is, listen for packets sent to this address).

```
   |   8    |  4 |  4 |                  112 bits                     |
   +------- -+----+----+-----------------------------------------------+
   |11111111|flgs|scop|                  group ID                     |
   +--------+----+----+-----------------------------------------------+


                                    +-+-+-+-+
      flgs is a set of 4 flags:     |0|0|0|T|
                                    +-+-+-+-+

      T = 0 indicates a permanently-assigned ("well-known") multicast
      address, assigned by the global internet numbering authority.


      T = 1 indicates a non-permanently-assigned ("transient")
      multicast address.

   scop is a 4-bit multicast scope value used to limit the scope of
   the multicast group.  The values are:

         0   reserved
         1   node-local scope
         2   link-local scope
         3   (unassigned)
         4   (unassigned)
         5   site-local scope
         6   (unassigned)
         7   (unassigned)
         8   organization-local scope
         9   (unassigned)
         A   (unassigned)
         B   (unassigned)
         C   (unassigned)
         D   (unassigned)
         E   global scope
         F   reserved


      group ID identifies the multicast group, either permanent or
      transient, within the given scope.
```

Figure 12.3 General format for IPv6 multicast addresses (from RFC 2373).

All-routers link-local multicast address. This is the address used to reach all routers (FF02:0:0:0:0:0:0:2) on the local link. All routers must subscribe to this group.

The solicited-node multicast address. Every node, as it gets an interface up on a network, must subscribe to the appropriate solicited-node multicast address that matches that interface's IPv6 address.

The link-local address. This is a unicast address that has a link-only scope. Figure 12.4, from RFC 2373, diagrams this address. All interfaces must have at least one link-local address. These addresses have the same interface ID as the globally unique IPv6 address but have a different network prefix, as shown in Figure 12.4. This address allows a node to identify itself (and be identified) uniquely on the local link without knowing the local link's IPv6 network prefix.

The unspecified address is a reserved address value (0:0:0:0:0:0:0:0). The unspecified address may never be used as a destination address, but it can be used as a source address when the sender has not yet determined its own address.

ICMP Messages for Neighbor Discovery

RFC 2461 defines five new ICMP (Internet Control Message Protocol) packet types, which, along with the multicast addresses described above, make it possible to achieve the neighbor discovery goals. The ICMP messages are used to request and respond to queries about routers and nodes in general, and to notify a node that a better router exists for a given route. The five ICMP packet types are as follows:

Router Advertisement. All routers periodically advertise that they are present on a link using this message. A Router Advertisement includes link and Internet parameters either by default in every transmission or by request (in response to a Router Solicitation message).

Router Solicitation. When a host's interface boots to the network, the host may request that routers on the link transmit their Router Advertisement messages *now* instead of waiting for the periodic transmission. This allows hosts to configure their interfaces with data sent by the router(s).

```
|   10   |
|  bits  |        54 bits          |           64 bits            |
+----------+-------------------------+------------------------------+
|1111111010|           0             |         interface ID         |
+----------+-------------------------+------------------------------+
```

Figure 12.4 The link-local address (from RFC 2373).

Neighbor Advertisement. This message is sent by a node in response to the Neighbor Solicitation message or when a link-layer address changes. It carries the link layer address of the node and can be used to map an IPv6 address to a link layer address.

Neighbor Solicitation. This message is sent by a node seeking a link layer address of a neighbor. The purpose may be to do address resolution, to verify a neighbor's reachability on a link layer address stored in the node's cache, or to detect duplicate addresses. In the last case, the node sends a solicitation out for the IPv6 address it wishes to use itself. If a response comes, the address is already in use.

Redirect. This message is used by a router to notify a host that there is another—better—first hop for that node to use to reach a particular destination.

As shown in the next section, an ICMP Neighbor Solicitation message, sent to the solicited-node multicast address, can replace the address resolution process defined for IPv4.

Neighbor Discovery Protocol Overview

The shape of the Neighbor Discovery protocol should be coming clear—at least for multicast-capable links. Each router advertises itself to the link by periodically multicasting a Router Advertisement packet. This packet indicates that the router is available and gives enough information for hosts to reach the router. Hosts on the link maintain a list of default routers on the link based on these advertisements, which each host receives via multicast. Router Advertisements each contain a list of prefixes that the router uses for determining whether a destination is local (that is, on the same link), and hosts on the link can use this information to determine what to do with packets (for example, when to attempt neighbor discovery and when to send a packet to a router).

The Router Advertisement also contains information relating to the way hosts can do autoconfiguration, indicating either that DHCPv6 should be used for stateful autoconfiguration or that stateless autoconfiguration should be used (as we see later in this chapter).

Individual nodes do address resolution with Neighbor Solicitation multicast message. This message is directed to the solicited-node multicast address (as described above) for the target address. The only node that should be a member of this multicast group is the target, and it replies to the Neighbor Solicitation multicast by sending a unicast Neighbor Advertisement message to the requesting node. Since the original Neighbor Solicitation message contains the link layer address of the requesting node, this single multicast request and the single unicast response are sufficient to get the two nodes communicating.

Neighbor Discovery works also as a duplicate address detection mechanism. When an interface to a link is brought up, the host can send a Neighbor Solicitation message to the solicited-node multicast address for the address it wishes to use. If some node on the link is already using that address, it responds, and the requesting host knows that the address is already in use.

Neighbor Unreachability Detection is another facet of Neighbor Discovery. One approach to detecting whether a neighbor or route is reachable is to use positive feedback from higher-layer protocols such as TCP (Transmission Control Protocol) or application protocols. However, this approach is not always possible, especially with message-oriented protocols such as UDP (User Datagram Protocol). In those cases, a host can send a unicast Neighbor Solicitation message to the destination (or router, for off-link routes). If the destination (or route) is still available the requesting host receives a unicast response from the target; otherwise, the requesting host can assume that the destination is no longer reachable.

Neighbor Discovery for IPv6 is hardly unique to Ethernet, but it is an important aspect of running IPv6 over Ethernet or any other similar link layer network. As we see later in the chapter, the IPv6 over Ethernet specification identifies Neighbor Discovery as an integral part of that standard.

IPv6 Stateless Autoconfiguration

RFC 2462, "IPv6 Stateless Address Autoconfiguration," is a draft standard that describes a mechanism by which an IPv6 node can configure its own address without having made any prior arrangement. Very simply, this is IP "plug and play." In a nutshell, IPv6 stateless autoconfiguration uses some of the mechanisms provided by neighbor discovery and the local link network prefix to make it possible for a node to determine whether it has a unique interface identifier on the link as well as to figure out the network prefix for the local link.

Networks may provide a sort of second-class citizenship to nodes using stateless autoconfiguration because there is no way to tell in advance who is responsible for these nodes: They might belong to a visiting vendor or they might be under control of an attacker attempting to subvert internal networks. However, stateless autoconfiguration provides an excellent mechanism for getting nodes up and running with a minimum of fuss.

Because stateless autoconfiguration depends on the interface having a unique identifier (the EUI-64 identifier, as described earlier in this chapter), it is particularly useful for Ethernet and other networks that use globally unique interface identifiers. These identifiers can be used as the basis for the link-unique identifier.

IPv6 over Ethernet

RFC 2464, "Transmission of IPv6 Packets over Ethernet Networks," is a proposed standard for transmitting IPv6 packets over Ethernet networks written by Matt Crawford of Fermilab. At seven pages, it is relatively short. It makes reference to neighbor discovery, stateless autoconfiguration, and EUI-64 addressing. Rather than summarizing it, we reproduce it here in full as was done in Chapter 11. The rest of this section appears in Courier font to indicate that it is taken verbatim and in full from RFC 2464.

Transmission of IPv6 Packets over Ethernet Networks

Status of This Memo

```
This document specifies an Internet standards track protocol for the
Internet community, and requests discussion and suggestions for
improvements.  Please refer to the current edition of the "Internet
Official Protocol Standards" (STD 1) for the standardization state
and status of this protocol.  Distribution of this memo is unlimited.
```

Copyright Notice

```
Copyright (C) The Internet Society (1998).  All Rights Reserved.
```

1. Introduction

```
This document specifies the frame format for transmission of IPv6
packets and the method of forming IPv6 link-local addresses and
statelessly autoconfigured addresses on Ethernet networks.  It also
```

specifies the content of the Source/Target Link-layer Address option used in Router Solicitation, Router Advertisement, Neighbor Solicitation, Neighbor Advertisement and Redirect messages when those messages are transmitted on an Ethernet.

This document replaces RFC 1972, "A Method for the Transmission of IPv6 Packets over Ethernet Networks", which will become historic.

The key words "MUST", "MUST NOT", "REQUIRED", "SHALL", "SHALL NOT", "SHOULD", "SHOULD NOT", "RECOMMENDED", "MAY", and "OPTIONAL" in this document are to be interpreted as described in [RFC 2119].

2. *Maximum Transmission Unit*

The default MTU size for IPv6 [IPV6] packets on an Ethernet is 1500 octets. This size may be reduced by a Router Advertisement [DISC] containing an MTU option which specifies a smaller MTU, or by manual configuration of each node. If a Router Advertisement received on an Ethernet interface has an MTU option specifying an MTU larger than 1500, or larger than a manually configured value, that MTU option may be logged to system management but must be otherwise ignored.

For purposes of this document, information received from DHCP is considered "manually configured" and the term Ethernet includes CSMA/CD and full-duplex subnetworks based on ISO/IEC 8802-3, with various data rates.

3. *Frame Format*

IPv6 packets are transmitted in standard Ethernet frames. The Ethernet header contains the Destination and Source Ethernet addresses and the Ethernet type code, which must contain the value 86DD hexadecimal. The data field contains the IPv6 header followed immediately by the payload, and possibly padding octets to meet the minimum frame size for the Ethernet link.

```
      0                   1
      0 1 2 3 4 5 6 7 8 9 0 1 2 3 4 5
     +-+-+-+-+-+-+-+-+-+-+-+-+-+-+-+-+
     |          Destination          |
     +-                             -+
     |           Ethernet            |
     +-                             -+
     |            Address            |
     +-+-+-+-+-+-+-+-+-+-+-+-+-+-+-+-+
     |             Source            |
     +-                             -+
     |           Ethernet            |
     +-                             -+
```

```
|              Address             |
+-+-+-+-+-+-+-+-+-+-+-+-+-+-+-+-+
|1 0 0 0 0 1 1 0 1 1 0 1 1 1 0 1|
+-+-+-+-+-+-+-+-+-+-+-+-+-+-+-+-+
|              IPv6                |
+-                             -+
|              header             |
+-                             -+
|              and                |
+-                             -+
/              payload ...         /
+-+-+-+-+-+-+-+-+-+-+-+-+-+-+-+-+
```

(Each tic mark represents one bit.)

4. *Stateless Autoconfiguration*

The Interface Identifier [AARCH] for an Ethernet interface is based
on the EUI-64 identifier [EUI64] derived from the interface's built-
in 48-bit IEEE 802 address. The EUI-64 is formed as follows.
(Canonical bit order is assumed throughout.)

The OUI of the Ethernet address (the first three octets) becomes the
company_id of the EUI-64 (the first three octets). The fourth and
fifth octets of the EUI are set to the fixed value FFFE hexadecimal.
The last three octets of the Ethernet address become the last three
octets of the EUI-64.

The Interface Identifier is then formed from the EUI-64 by
complementing the "Universal/Local" (U/L) bit, which is the next-to-
lowest order bit of the first octet of the EUI-64. Complementing
this bit will generally change a 0 value to a 1, since an interface's
built-in address is expected to be from a universally administered
address space and hence have a globally unique value. A universally
administered IEEE 802 address or an EUI-64 is signified by a 0 in the
U/L bit position, while a globally unique IPv6 Interface Identifier
is signified by a 1 in the corresponding position. For further
discussion on this point, see [AARCH].

For example, the Interface Identifier for an Ethernet interface whose
built-in address is, in hexadecimal,

                    34-56-78-9A-BC-DE

would be

                    36-56-78-FF-FE-9A-BC-DE.

A different MAC address set manually or by software should not be
used to derive the Interface Identifier. If such a MAC address must

be used, its global uniqueness property should be reflected in the
value of the U/L bit.

An IPv6 address prefix used for stateless autoconfiguration [ACONF]
of an Ethernet interface must have a length of 64 bits.

5. Link-Local Addresses

The IPv6 link-local address [AARCH] for an Ethernet interface is
formed by appending the Interface Identifier, as defined above, to
the prefix FE80::/64.

```
    10 bits              54 bits                   64 bits
  +----------+----------------------+--------------------------+
  |1111111010|       (zeros)        |    Interface Identifier  |
  +----------+----------------------+--------------------------+
```

6. Address Mapping—Unicast

The procedure for mapping IPv6 unicast addresses into Ethernet link-
layer addresses is described in [DISC]. The Source/Target Link-layer
Address option has the following form when the link layer is
Ethernet.

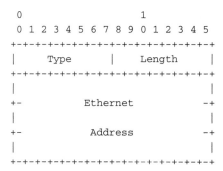

```
                      0                   1
                      0 1 2 3 4 5 6 7 8 9 0 1 2 3 4 5
                     +-+-+-+-+-+-+-+-+-+-+-+-+-+-+-+-+
                     |     Type      |    Length     |
                     +-+-+-+-+-+-+-+-+-+-+-+-+-+-+-+-+
                     |                               |
                     +-        Ethernet            -+
                     |                               |
                     +-        Address             -+
                     |                               |
                     +-+-+-+-+-+-+-+-+-+-+-+-+-+-+-+-+
```

Option fields:

Type   1 for Source Link-layer address.
            2 for Target Link-layer address.

Length   1 (in units of 8 octets).

Ethernet Address
            The 48 bit Ethernet IEEE 802 address, in canonical bit
            order. This is the address the interface currently
            responds to, and may be different from the built-in
            address used to derive the Interface Identifier.

7. Address Mapping—Multicast

An IPv6 packet with a multicast destination address DST, consisting of the sixteen octets DST[1] through DST[16], is transmitted to the Ethernet multicast address whose first two octets are the value 3333 hexadecimal and whose last four octets are the last four octets of DST.

```
+-+-+-+-+-+-+-+-+-+-+-+-+-+-+-+-+
|0 0 1 1 0 0 1 1|0 0 1 1 0 0 1 1|
+-+-+-+-+-+-+-+-+-+-+-+-+-+-+-+-+
|    DST[13]     |    DST[14]    |
+-+-+-+-+-+-+-+-+-+-+-+-+-+-+-+-+
|    DST[15]     |    DST[16]    |
+-+-+-+-+-+-+-+-+-+-+-+-+-+-+-+-+
```

8. Differences from RFC 1972

The following are the functional differences between this specification and RFC 1972.

The Address Token, which was a node's 48-bit MAC address, is replaced with the Interface Identifier, which is 64 bits in length and based on the EUI-64 format [EUI64]. An IEEE-defined mapping exists from 48-bit MAC addresses to EUI-64 form.

A prefix used for stateless autoconfiguration must now be 64 bits long rather than 80. The link-local prefix is also shortened to 64 bits.

9. Security Considerations

The method of derivation of Interface Identifiers from MAC addresses is intended to preserve global uniqueness when possible. However, there is no protection from duplication through accident or forgery.

10. References

[AARCH] Hinden, R. and S. Deering "IP Version 6 Addressing Architecture", RFC 2373, July 1998.

[ACONF] Thomson, S. and T. Narten, "IPv6 Stateless Address Autoconfiguration", RFC 2462, December 1998.

[DISC] Narten, T., Nordmark, E. and W. Simpson, "Neighbor Discovery for IP Version 6 (IPv6)", RFC 2461, December 1998.

[EUI64] "Guidelines For 64-bit Global Identifier (EUI-64)", http://standards.ieee.org/db/oui/tutorials/EUI64.html

[IPV6] Deering, S. and R. Hinden, "Internet Protocol, Version 6
(IPv6) Specification", RFC 2460, December 1998.

[RFC 2119] Bradner, S., "Key words for use in RFCs to Indicate
Requirement Levels", BCP 14, RFC 2119, March 1997.

11. Author's Address

Matt Crawford
Fermilab MS 368
PO Box 500
Batavia, IL 60510
USA

Phone: +1 630 840-3461
EMail: crawdad@fnal.gov

Reading List

Table 12.1 contains RFCs pertaining to IPv6 over Ethernet. Although many documents cite a URL for an IEEE tutorial on the EUI-64 standard for 64-bit global address, that page is long gone. A better resource is available in appendix A of RFC 2373.

Table 12.1 RFCs Relating to IPv6 over Ethernet

RFC	STATUS	TITLE
RFC 2462	Draft Standard	IPv6 Stateless Address Autoconfiguration
RFC 2461	Draft Standard	Neighbor Discover for IP Version 6
RFC 2460	Draft Standard	Internet Protocol, Version 6 (IPv6) Specification
RFC 2464	Proposed Standard	Transmission of IPv6 Packets over Ethernet Networks
RFC 2375	Informational	IPv6 Multicast Address Assignments
RFC 1981	Proposed Standard	Path MTU Discovery for IP version 6
RFC 2373	Proposed Standard	IP Version 6 Addressing Architecture
RFC 2374	Proposed Standard	An IPv6 Aggregatable Global Unicast Address Format

CHAPTER 13

Multicast, Broadcast, and Ethernet

Baseband Ethernet can be likened to a high school cafeteria with the students representing individual nodes, the public address system representing the cable, and announcements standing in for Ethernet frames. When the principal makes an announcement, she starts out by stating to whom she is sending the announcement. When she announces "Bobby Smith, please report to the school secretary," everyone can hear the announcement, but only Bobby Smith pays attention to it (and presumably takes action on it).

The medium in this example is a broadcast medium. Unicasts, announcements intended for a single recipient, are broadcast, and all stations (students) other than the intended recipient ignore them. True broadcasts, on the other hand, are also broadcast over the network medium (public address system). Instead of being addressed to a single recipient, broadcasts are prefaced by some indicator that everyone should pay attention: The principal begins the announcement by saying, "All students please report to the gymnasium after school for class photos." Instead of hearing an individual student's name and then ignoring the message, all students in the cafeteria listen to the broadcast and take action on it (or explicitly ignore it).

A multicast is a point-to-multipoint transmission. This means that the message originates from a single node but is intended for more than one recipient. In our cafeteria example, a multicast message might take the form of "all members of the chess club" or "all seniors" or "anyone who missed class photo day" or any other classification to which a node (or student) either does or does not belong. Members of the group pay attention; nonmembers ignore the message.

In this chapter, we discuss how IP broadcast and IP multicast work, and how they are mapped to Ethernet and IEEE 802.3 networks.

IP Broadcast

In this section, we look at the mechanics of IP broadcast and discuss how it is mapped to Ethernet and IEEE 802.3 networks. We introduce the issues related to IP broadcast as described in STD 5, which consists of various specifications for the Internet Protocol (IP) and related standards. Table 13.1 lists the components of this standard.

IP Broadcast Standards

RFC 919 (STD-5), "Broadcasting Internet Datagrams," and RFC 922, "Broadcasting Internet Datagrams in the Presence of Subnets," were both published in 1984. The authors justify broadcast packets on several grounds. For one thing, it is argued that "Most common local area networks do support broadcast; for example, Ethernet, ChaosNet, token ring networks, etc." Of course, there are important newer network types such as ATM that do not support broadcasts, but ATM was not even on the horizon in 1984.

Table 13.1 Components of STD-5

RFC	TITLE
RFC 1112	Host Extensions for IP Multicasting
RFC 950	Internet Standard Subnetting Procedure
RFC 922	Broadcasting Internet Datagrams in the Presence of Subnets
RFC 919	Broadcasting Internet Datagrams
RFC 792	Internet Control Message Protocol (ICMP)
RFC 791	Internet Protocol

The authors also state that "Broadcasts are useful when a host needs to find information without knowing exactly what other host can supply it..." The idea is that a broadcast transmission attracts the attention of an appropriate host, which then responds with the information desired. This, of course, is the principle on which ARP is built. They continue, "...or when a host wants to provide information to a large set of hosts in a timely manner." This refers to things such as router reachability or node management information.

Broadcast Classes

RFC 922 defines different broadcast classes. The classes are included here as defined in RFC 919 (in Courier font) followed by a brief explanation:

```
- Single-destination datagrams broadcast on the local hardware
  net: A datagram is destined for a specific IP host, but the
  sending host broadcasts it at the data link layer, perhaps to
  avoid having to do routing.  Since this is not an IP broadcast,
  the IP layer is not involved, except that a host should discard
  datagram not meant for it without becoming flustered (i.e.,
  printing an error message).
```

Such a packet would be broadcast at the link layer (for example, sent to the Ethernet broadcast address), but once it unwrapped the link layer headers the node would find an IP packet directed to a unicast address. In this case, the destination node recognizes the packet as its own, while all the other nodes on the network (who have also unwrapped the frame) discard the packet. This type of broadcasting is frowned on because it wastes network resources as well as resources on every node attached to the network.

```
- Broadcast to all hosts on the local hardware net: A
  distinguished value for the host-number part of the IP address
  denotes broadcast instead of a specific host.  The receiving IP
  layer must be able to recognize this address as well as its own.
  However, it might still be useful to distinguish at higher
  levels between broadcasts and non-broadcasts, especially in
  gateways.  This is the most useful case of broadcast; it allows
  a host to discover gateways without wired-in tables, it is the
  basis for address resolution protocols, and it is also useful
  for accessing such utilities as name servers, time servers,
  etc., without requiring wired-in addresses.
```

The "all-ones" broadcast address, 255.255.255.255, is used to send broadcasts to the local link. Host network software, when seeing this address on an IP packet destination, encapsulates the packet in a link layer frame addressed to the link broadcast address. This is also known as a limited broadcast. These packets are never forwarded across a router beyond the local link. This is the most commonly encountered type of IP broadcast.

```
- Broadcast to all hosts on a remote hardware network: It is
  occasionally useful to send a broadcast to all hosts on a
  non-local network; for example, to find the latest version of a
  hostname database, to bootload a host on a subnet without a
  bootserver, or to monitor the timeservers on the subnet.  This
  case is the same as local-network broadcasts; the datagram is
  routed by normal mechanisms until it reaches a gateway attached
  to the destination hardware network, at which point it is
  broadcast.  This class of broadcasting is also known as
  "directed broadcasting", or quaintly as sending a "letter bomb".
```

There are three types of directed broadcasts: net-directed broadcasts, which are intended to be received by all nodes on a remote network; subnet-directed broadcasts, which are intended to be received by all nodes on a subnet of a remote network; and all-subnets-directed broadcasts, which are intended to be received by all nodes on a subnetted network. All-subnets-directed broadcasts are discussed separately. The standards require intermediate routers to forward directed broadcasts to the destination network, where the destination router can be configured to drop them—although the default is for routers to forward those broadcasts. In general, such directed broadcasts tend to generate more trouble than they are worth. If a router forwards directed broadcasts onto a network, denial of service attacks against the network are possible.

```
- Broadcast to all hosts on a subnetted IP network (Multi-subnet
  broadcasts): A distinguished value for the subnet-number part of
  the IP address is used to denote "all subnets".  Broadcasts to
  all hosts of a remote subnetted IP network are done just as
  directed broadcasts to a single subnet.
```

RFC 1812, "Requirements for IP Version 4 Routers," notes that the all-subnets-directed broadcast algorithm is "broken." Further, the authors note: "To the knowledge of the working group, the facility was never implemented or deployed, and is now relegated to the dustbin of history." Enough said about this.

```
- Broadcast to the entire Internet: This is probably not useful,
  and almost certainly not desirable.
```

Broadcast to the entire Internet is not only definitely not useful, as routing and other application protocols are far more efficient mechanisms to distribute information across the Internet, but absolutely not desirable. Every improper Internet broadcast would consume massive volumes of network resources if they were allowed. It is so clearly not a good idea that there is no way to express an all-Internet broadcast address.

IP Broadcast Addresses

Although most platforms have used the all-ones (255.255.255.255) addresses to denote an IP broadcast, this has not always been universal. RFC 1812 identifies the all-zeroes forms as obsolete. Prior to that, the all-zeroes address (0.0.0.0) was used by some systems to indicate an IP broadcast.

Table 13.2 shows some of the different broadcast address formats that are currently acceptable.

IP Broadcast over Ethernet/IEEE 802.3

The Ethernet/IEEE 802.3 broadcast address is also all-ones: 0xFF:FF:FF: FF:FF:FF.

Table 13.2 Acceptable IP Broadcast Addresses

ADDRESS	BROADCAST TYPE
255.255.255.255	Local link broadcast address. Never forwarded.
[Class A network ID].255.255.255	Net-directed Class A broadcast address. Forwarded by default, but forwarding can be turned off at the destination network.
[Class B network ID].255.255	Net-directed Class B broadcast address. Forwarded by default, but forwarding can be turned off at the destination network.
[Class C network ID].255	Net-directed Class C broadcast address. Forwarded by default, but forwarding can be turned off at the destination network.
[Class B network ID].[subnet ID].255	Example of a subnet-directed Class B broadcast address. Forwarded by default, but forwarding can be turned off at the destination network.

IP broadcasts over Ethernet and IEEE 802.3 are quite simple:

- If a node receives an Ethernet/IEEE 802.3 frame with the destination 0xFF:FF:FF:FF:FF:FF, the node reads the frame and passes it up the protocol stack to be unwrapped.

- If a node wishes to send an IP—or any other network layer—broadcast to the local Ethernet/IEEE 802.3 link, the node encapsulates the packet inside a frame addressed to 0xFF:FF:FF:FF:FF:FF.

IP Multicast

As part of STD-5, RFC 1112, "Host Extensions for IP Multicasting," defines how IP multicasting works. Multicast is a sort of smart broadcast. Instead of sending a frame to everyone on a network (whether it be an entire internetwork or just the local link), multicast allows you to address a packet to a group address and then have it delivered only to members of the group.

IP multicast requires that you solve two problems. First, you must be able to deliver packets addressed to a multicast address to all the members of the multicast group on the local link. Second, you must be able to deliver packets addressed to a multicast address to all the members of the multicast group across multiple local links or over an internetwork. The first problem, at least for Ethernet and IEEE 802.3, is relatively simple to accomplish. The second problem, which requires multicast routing protocols, is beyond the scope of this book.

In this section, we provide a quick overview to IP multicast addressing and group membership, followed by a discussion of the Internet Group Multicast Protocol (IGMP). We finish this section by examining the mechanisms by which IP multicast is mapped onto Ethernet, as documented in RFC 1112.

IP Multicast Addresses and Groups

The IP standards define Class D addresses as multicast addresses. Class D addresses have the high-order four bits of the address set to 1110 and therefore are any addresses in the range of 224.0.0.0 through 239.255.255.255. A multicast address serves a group, all members of which accept packets sent to that address. The address 224.0.0.0 is unassigned, and the address 224.0.0.1 is assigned to a permanent group that includes all hosts on the local ("this") subnet.

Table 13.3 lists some reserved multicast addresses, taken from the IANA Web site (http://www.isi.edu/in-notes/iana/assignments/multicast-addresses). This table lists addresses reserved in the first block (224.0.0.0 through 224.0.0.255, to be used for routing purposes only) of Class D addresses as well as some other, possibly interesting, reserved addresses and blocks. The first block includes the well-known multicast addresses for all hosts and all routers on this subnet (224.0.0.2). Anyone may reserve one or more multicast addresses by application.

The problem of how to route multicast packets is very interesting, but not within the scope of this book. We cover the problem of how to associate an IP multicast address with an Ethernet/IEEE 802.3 multicast address in the next section.

Table 13.3   Reserved IP Multicast Addresses (from www.iana.org)

ADDRESS (OR ADDRESS BLOCK)	RESERVED FOR
224.0.0.0	Base Address (Reserved)
224.0.0.1	All Systems on this Subnet
224.0.0.2	All Routers on this Subnet
224.0.0.3	Unassigned
224.0.0.4	DVMRP Routers
224.0.0.5	OSPFIGP All Routers
224.0.0.6	OSPFIGP Designated Routers
224.0.0.7	ST Routers
224.0.0.8	ST Hosts
224.0.0.9	RIP2 Routers
224.0.0.10	IGRP Routers
224.0.0.11	Mobile-Agents
224.0.0.12	DHCP Server / Relay Agent
224.0.0.13	All PIM Routers
224.0.0.14	RSVP-ENCAPSULATION
224.0.0.15	All-cbt-routers
224.0.0.16	designated-sbm
224.0.0.17	All-sbms

Continues

Table 13.3   Reserved IP Multicast Addresses (from www.iana.org) *(Continued)*

ADDRESS (OR ADDRESS BLOCK)	RESERVED FOR
224.0.0.18	VRRP
224.0.0.19-224.0.0.255	Unassigned
224.0.1.39	Cisco-rp-announce
224.0.1.40	Cisco-rp-discovery
224.0.12.000-224.0.12.063	Microsoft and MSNBC
224.0.18.000-224.0.18.255	Dow Jones
224.0.19.000-224.0.19.063	Walt Disney Company
224.0.252.000-224.0.252.255	Domain Scoped Group
224.0.253.000-224.0.253.255	Report Group
224.0.254.000-224.0.254.255	Query Group
224.0.255.000-224.0.255.255	Border Routers
224.1.0.0-224.1.255.255	ST Multicast Groups
224.2.0.0-224.2.127.253	Multimedia Conference Calls
224.2.127.254	SAPv1 Announcements
224.2.127.255	SAPv0 Announcements (deprecated)
224.2.128.0-224.2.255.255	SAP Dynamic Assignments
224.252.0.0-224.255.255.255	DIS transient groups
225.0.0.0-225.255.255.255	MALLOC (temp - renew 12/99)
232.0.0.0-232.255.255.255	VMTP transient groups
233.0.0.0-233.255.255.255	Static Allocations (temp - renew 6/00)
239.000.000.000-239.255.255.255	Administratively Scoped
239.000.000.000-239.063.255.255	Reserved
239.064.000.000-239.127.255.255	Reserved
239.128.000.000-239.191.255.255	Reserved
239.192.000.000-239.251.255.255	Organization-Local Scope
239.252.000.000-239.252.255.255	Site-Local Scope (reserved)
239.253.000.000-239.253.255.255	Site-Local Scope (reserved)
239.254.000.000-239.254.255.255	Site-Local Scope (reserved)
239.255.000.000-239.255.255.255	Site-Local Scope

Mapping IP to Ethernet Multicast

Support for IP multicast, according to RFC 1112, is available in three levels. Level 0 offers no support for IP multicast; Level 1 supports sending multicast packets but not receiving them; Level 2 offers full support for both sending and receiving multicast packets. Because Ethernet was such an important link layer protocol for the Internet at the time it was published, RFC 1112 discusses implementation of multicast support for Ethernet. That discussion is split into two parts, the first covering extensions necessary to send multicast over Ethernet and the second covering extensions necessary to receive multicast packets.

Sending IP Multicast over Ethernet

RFC 1112 states that it is not necessary to add anything to the local network service interface because the IP module on the host just specifies the multicast group address instead of a unicast address when it sends a multicast packet.

Ethernet supports multicast packets at the link layer, and RFC 1112 specifies that the Ethernet local network module of the host needs only to be able to map IP multicast group addresses to Ethernet multicast addresses in order to support multicast transmission.

As RFC 1112 puts it:

```
An IP host group address is mapped to an Ethernet multicast address
by placing the low-order 23-bits of the IP address into the low-order
23 bits of the Ethernet multicast address 01-00-5E-00-00-00 (hex).
Because there are 28 significant bits in an IP host group address,
more than one host group address may map to the same Ethernet
multicast address.
```

Thus, sending a multicast over Ethernet is a very simple matter. Only minimal programming is necessary to convert a nonmulticast IP over Ethernet implementation to a level 1 compliant multicast implementation.

Receiving IP Multicast over Ethernet

In order to receive IP multicast packets, the local network service interface has to add two operations: one to allow the host to join a multicast group and the other to allow the host to leave a multicast group. Each of these operations is defined to take an IP multicast group address as a required parameter. It is left to the local network module to map the IP multicast group address to an Ethernet (or other link layer) multicast address. The host's local network module must not accept frames sent out on the interface by that same host.

Hosts on the local link subscribe to the IP multicast address simply by accepting Ethernet multicasts sent to the IP-to-Ethernet mapped address described above. The lack of a one-to-one mapping of IP multicast addresses to Ethernet multicast addresses raises some potential problems. One problem arises when a network contain subscribers to two or more different IP multicast groups that share a single Ethernet multicast address. In this case, each host has to process all the Ethernet multicasts that might be carrying IP packets addressed to the multicast group of interest. When the Ethernet frame is stripped away, the host checks the IP multicast address and if it is the right one (identifying the IP multicast group to which the host belongs), the host accepts the IP packet. Otherwise, it discards the packet.

Another problem can crop up if a host has to subscribe to many IP multicast groups. Some interfaces are not able to keep track of and monitor very many Ethernet multicast addresses. When the number of groups a host belongs to exceeds the number of addresses it can track, it must stop trying to listen only to selected multicast addresses and must monitor all Ethernet multicasts. In this way, it is guaranteed to receive all multicasts addressed to groups to which the host belongs as well as all multicasts addressed to other groups.

Reading List

Table 13.4 lists RFCs that describe network management issues pertaining to Ethernet RFCs cited in this chapter. The reading list for Chapter 7 is also helpful for understanding the MIB and managed object issues discussed in this chapter.

Table 13.4 Broadcast and Multicast RFCs

RFC	STATUS	TITLE
RFC 791	STD 5	Internet Protocol
RFC 792	STD 5	Internet Control Message Protocol (ICMP)
RFC 919	STD 5	Broadcasting Internet Datagrams
RFC 922	STD 5	Broadcasting Internet Datagrams in the Presence of Subnets
RFC 950	STD 5	Internet Standard Subnetting Procedure
RFC 1112	STD 5	Host Extensions for IP Multicasting
RFC 1122	STD 3	Requirements for Internet Hosts— Communication Layers
RFC 1812	Proposed Standard	Requirements for IP Version 4 Routers

Ethernet MIBs

In this chapter, we look at Ethernet management issues covered by Internet standards. Very broadly, these can be characterized as belonging to one of two categories: those specifications that define managed objects and MIBs related to Ethernet and those defining managed objects and MIBs related to IEEE 802.3 network devices.

We've already discussed Internet standards for network management in Chapter 7. After taking a brief look at managed objects and MIBs in general as well as the Interfaces Group MIB, we summarize the standards work done on Ethernet and IEEE 802.3-related managed objects and MIBs. We also review early work done on using SNMP directly over Ethernet and the Ethernet Internet MIB.

Managed Objects and MIBs

MIB and managed objects specifications tend to be quite long, if only because they must reproduce lengthy ASN.1 definitions. Rather than attempting to provide all the details of every MIB, in this section we briefly introduce some of the MIB and managed objects relevant to Ethernet and IEEE 802.3 networks.

The Interfaces Group MIB

It is a convenience to be able to talk about IP being the network layer protocol that sits on top of some monolithic link layer protocol, but that is not always correct. The proposed standard RFC 2233, "The Interfaces Group MIB Using SMIv2," documents mechanisms for representing more complicated interface situations and for storing and manipulating management data relating to these situations.

Complications in the interfaces table of MIB-II arise from a number of areas. Some link layer technologies make extensive use of sublayers, such as ATM. Should interface management information be limited to the ATM Adaptation Layer, or should a separate interface entry be added to a table for each virtual circuit associated with a station?

Managed Objects for Ethernet-Like Interface Types

Currently, STD 50 is contained within RFC 1643, "Definitions of Managed Objects for the Ethernet-like Interface Types." However, RFC 2538 has the same title, but is a proposed standard. RFC 2358 makes obsolete a third RFC, RFC 1650, "Definitions of Managed Objects for the Ethernet-like Interface Types Using SMIv2." In fact, RFC 2358 builds in large part on both RFC 1643 and RFC 1650 and extends the specification to support 100Mbps Ethernet. These specifications rely on the ASN.1 syntax as do all other MIB and managed objects definitions.

RFC 2358 defines managed objects for interfaces to Ethernet-like media. "Ethernet-like" means media that share attributes of Ethernet and include regular Ethernet as well as IEEE 802.3 and StarLAN networks. This specification does not, however, provide for layering. Should any layering be necessary—for example, if it is necessary to manage at the IEEE 802.2 layer or at an Ethernet transceiver layer—RFC 2358 explicitly does not define mechanisms for dealing with such layers. The authors do, however, indicate that in the event that these layers become necessary, they must be specified in terms of requirements that go beyond RFC 2358. Likewise, since Ethernet-like networks don't support virtual circuits, RFC 2358 does not specify any objects for them.

Table 14.1 lists all the objects defined in RFC 2358, with explanations taken from RFC 2358 and from RFC 2233, "The Interfaces Group MIB Using SMIv2."

Table 14.1 Managed Objects for Ethernet-Like Interfaces (from RFC 2358 and RFC 2233)

OBJECT	DESCRIPTION
ifIndex	Interface index. Each Ethernet-like interface on a host is represented by an ifEntry value.
ifDescr	Interface description. A text-string value that contains information about the interface, specifically the manufacturer and product name and version numbers for the interface hardware and software.
ifType	Interface type. For Ethernet-like interfaces, valid values here are EthernetCsmacd(6), iso88023Csmacd(7), and starLan(11). There exist values that could go in this object specifying Fast Ethernet, but the authors of RFC 2358 assert that Ethernet is Ethernet and should use the generic Ethernet identifier.
ifMTU	Maximum transmission unit (MTU) for the interface. 1500 octets.
ifSpeed	Interface speed. The current operational speed of the interface in bits per second. For example, for traditional Ethernet, this would be 10,000,000 (10Mbps); for 100Mbps Ethernet, this would be 100,000,000. If the interface supports autonegotiation and a speed has not yet been negotiated, this should contain the maximum speed that the interface can support. If the interface operates in full-duplex mode, this value must not be doubled.
ifPhysAddress	The interface's physical (or lower layer) address. For Ethernet-like interfaces, this is the MAC address.
ifAdminStatus	Per RFC 2233, this is "The desired state of the interface." This object can contain the values up, down, or testing.
ifOperStatus	The operational state of the interface. RFC 2233 defines values that can be used here, including up, down, testing, unknown, dormant (not an option for Ethernet-like interfaces), notPresent (some part is missing), and lowerLayerDown (down due to problems with a lower layer).
ifLastChange	The value of the system up-time object when the interface entered its current operational state. In other words, this is the last time the interface changed status.
ifInOctets	The number of inbound octets in valid MAC frames (octets received) on this interface.
ifInUcastPkts	The number of inbound unicast packets received on the interface.
ifInDiscards	The number of inbound unicast packets with nothing detectable wrong with them, but that are discarding anyway (for example, to free up buffer space).
ifInErrors	The total of all the errors totaled up by the objects tracking alignment errors, frame check sequence (FCS) errors, frames that were too long, frames with internal errors, and symbol errors.

Continues

Table 14.1   Managed Objects for Ethernet-Like Interfaces (from RFC 2358 and RFC 2233) (Continued)

OBJECT	DESCRIPTION
ifInUnknownProtos	The number of inbound packets that were discarded because they used unknown protocols.
ifOutOctets	Number of outbound octets transmitted in valid MAC frames from this interface.
ifOutUcastPkts	Number of unicast packets transmitted on the interface.
ifOutDiscards	Number of packets discarded despite there being nothing wrong detected with them. One possible reason for discarding a packet might be to free buffer space.
ifOutErrors	The total number of outbound error frames, including test errors, collisions, transmit errors, and carrier sense errors.
ifName	A text name for the interface, with local significance (for example, lan0 or eth1).
ifInMulticastPkts	A 32-bit counter tracking the number of inbound multicast packets received.
ifInBroadcastPkts	A 32-bit counter tracking the number of inbound broadcast packets received.
ifOutMulticastPkts	A 32-bit counter tracking the number of outbound multicast packets sent.
ifOutBroadcastPkts	A 32-bit counter tracking the number of outbound broadcast packets sent.
ifHCInOctets ifHCOutOctets	Counters that track the number of inbound and outbound octets. ifHCOutOctets and ifHCInOctets are 64-bit counters, required for Ethernet-like interfaces that operate at 20Mbps or faster. The longer counters are necessary because a 32-bit counter would cycle after only about 4 billion packets. This is not a problem for 10Mbps Ethernet, where even at maximum rates an interface would need an hour or so to roll the counter over; however, the 32-bit counter is not enough for 100Mbps or gigabit Ethernet, which could cause the counter to turn over as quickly as minutes or even seconds.
ifHCInUcastPkts ifHCInMulticastPkts ifHCInBroadcastPkts ifHCOutUcastPkts ifHCOutMulticastPkts ifHCOutBroadcastPkts	These are 64-bit counters tracking the number of inbound and outbound unicast, multicast, and broadcast packets transmitted/received from/to the interface. These countersare required for interface types capable of operating at 640Mbps or faster, for the same reasons that the octet counters must use 64 bits for higher bit rate interfaces.

Table 14.1 *(Continued)*

OBJECT	DESCRIPTION
ifLinkUpDownTrapEnable	This object is used to let manager generate traps only on a particular sublayer. For Ethernet-like interfaces and any other interfaces which don't use sublayers, it is enabled by default.
ifHighSpeed	This indicates the current bandwidth in units of millions of bits per second. For Ethernet-like interfaces, it is generally limited to values of 10 or 100 (for 10Mbps or 100Mbps Ethernet).
ifPromiscuousMode	Indicates whether the interface accepts any packets sent on the local link (in which case the value here is true) or not (false). The value of this object does not affect whether the interface is capable of receiving broadcasts and multicasts that it should receive.
ifConnectorPresent	This indicates whether the interface has a physical connector.
ifAlias	Contains an alias for the interface that remains constant over time to be used for administrative or management purposes.
ifCounterDiscontinuityTime	This indicates the time since the last discontinuity (an existing counter value was dropped and a new one added) occurred in one of the interface counters.
ifStackHigherLayer ifStackLowerLayer ifStackStatus	RFC 2358 makes no provision for sublayers, but the interface stack table (entries that consist of these objects) is mandatory for all systems, per RFC 2233. The higher and lower layer objects are set to 0 for Ethernet-like interfaces.
ifRcvAddressAddress ifRcvAddressStatus ifRcvAddressType	These objects are part of the ifRcvAddressTable object and contain all the IEEE 802.3 addresses (unicast, multicast, and broadcast) for which the interface receives packets. This table is not intended to maintain unicast addresses for Ethernet bridge devices, however.

Managed Objects for IEEE 802.3

In addition to the specification for managed objects for Ethernet-like networks, there are additional MIBs and managed object definitions specifications relating to IEEE 802.3. For example, RFC 2239, "Definitions of Managed Objects for IEEE 802.3 Medium Attachment Units (MAUs) Using SMIv2," is a proposed standard that defines managed objects for the medium attachment units (MAUs) that link the Ethernet interface with the Ethernet cable.

All Ethernet-like interfaces must support the mauModIfCompl object defined in RFC 2239. This object specifies compliance for MAUs attached to interfaces. It is used to indicate whether the interface is capable of doing 100Mbps, whether it has external jacks, whether it supports managed autonegotiation, whether it is a broadband MAU, and whether the MAU is attached directly to the interface.

The MAU type, as specified in RFC 2239, indicates not just the media type but also whether the interface is operating in full- or half-duplex mode. Since this information is not available anywhere in the Ethernet-like interface managed objects, support for the MAU MIB is required.

More IEEE 802.3 managed objects are specified in another proposed standard, RFC 2108, "Definitions of Managed Objects for IEEE 802.3 Repeater Devices Using SMIv2," which provides tools for managing IEEE 802.3 repeaters and repeater-like devices. Specifically, RFC 2108 defines mechanisms for tracking management information for the multiple ports of a repeater.

SNMP over Ethernet

SNMP, as usually defined, uses UDP for its transport protocol and IP as its network layer protocol. For SNMP to be useful in an internetwork environment, it must have a network layer protocol to carry it across link boundaries. However, there is no reason that SNMP (or almost any network application) could not be carried over some other protocol. RFC 1089, "SNMP over Ethernet," is an experimental (and very short) description of how SNMP messages can be encapsulated directly into Ethernet frames, bypassing IP.

By defining an EtherType value of 33100 (decimal) or 0x814C (hexadecimal) for SNMP traffic, you can encapsulate SNMP messages directly into Ethernet/IEEE 802.3 frames. This approach was thought to be of use in networks and for network devices that do not implement any higher-layer protocols for carrying network traffic.

Reading List

Table 14.2 lists RFCs that describe network management issues pertaining to Ethernet. RFCs cited in the reading list for Chapter 7 are also helpful for understanding the MIB and managed object issues discussed in this chapter.

Table 14.2 Ethernet and Management RFCs

RFC	STATUS	TITLE
RFC 1089	Experimental	SNMP over Ethernet
RFC 1369	Informational	Implementation Notes and Experience for The Internet Ethernet MIB
RFC 1515	Proposed Standard (but superseded by RFC 2239)	Definitions of Managed Objects for IEEE 802.3 Medium Attachment Units (MAUs)
RFC 1643	STD 50	Definitions of Managed Objects for the Ethernet-Like Interface Types
RFC 2011	Proposed Standard	SNMPv2 Management Information Base for the Internet Protocol Using SMIv2
RFC 2108	Proposed Standard	Definitions of Managed Objects for IEEE 802.3 Repeater Devices Using SMIv2
RFC 2233	Proposed Standard	The Interfaces Group MIB Using SMIv2
RFC 2239	Proposed Standard	Definitions of Managed Objects for IEEE 802.3 Medium Attachment Units (MAUs) Using SMIv2
RFC 2358	Proposed Standard	Definitions of Managed Objects for the Ethernet-Like Interface Types

The Future of Ethernet and IP

Ethernet turned out to be just the thing to help get IP started: an open standard for local area networking. Ethernet made it possible to connect lots of different types of computers and other devices to the same local link. IP made it possible for all those nodes to communicate with each other across interconnected local area networks. The histories of the development and use of Ethernet and the Internet Protocol twine around each other and will continue to do so for as long as IP runs over Ethernet.

Ethernet is a well-understood, mature, and widely deployed link layer protocol. IP over Ethernet is also well understood and widely deployed. There is relatively little to be discovered about the way IP runs over Ethernet. There are no active IP over Ethernet working groups anymore. The IPv6 over Ethernet specification came out of the IPng group. Most research and development activity relating to link layers focuses on the latest new technologies. ATM is one, while the FireWire (IEEE 1394) standard for communicating with multimedia and other nontraditional devices is another.

Despite the commercial introduction and market acceptance first of 100Mbps Ethernet and, more recently, of gigabit Ethernet, the principals remain largely the same as they were when 10Mbps Ethernet was considered pretty fast. This is not to say that no more Internet standards will be defined that relate to Ethernet, but rather that Ethernet standards, vis à vis the Internet, are largely in maintenance mode rather than active development mode.

For example, there is one Internet-Draft in the pipeline that discusses the use of gratuitous ARP. Rather than breaking new ground, it fixes a flaw in the original specifications that described gratuitous ARP. In the original, there is no formal specification of what a host should do when it discovers that the IP address it wishes to register is already in use by another node. As any IP network engineer knows, duplicate IP addresses are both one of the more common network problems and one of the more difficult to quickly diagnose and solve. The gratuitous ARP extensions draft is certainly useful, but hardly earth shattering.

Ultimately, something better, faster, cheaper, and easier is certain to come along and replace Ethernet. Until then, however, we have plenty of time to work with this familiar standard.

Reading List

Table 15.1 contains a list of some Web sites that are likely to have further information about new developments pertaining to Ethernet and IP.

Table 15.1   Web Sites with Ethernet/IEEE Standard Information

URL	ORGANIZATION	DESCRIPTION
www.ietf.org/html.charters/wg-dir.html	IETF	Active IETF working groups page. Future work affecting or affected by Ethernet might occur in the Internet, Operations and Management, or Routing areas.
grouper.ieee.org/groups/802/index.html	IEEE 802 LAN/MAN Standards Committee	Information about the creation and development of local/metropolitan area networking standards by IEEE.
www.gigabit-Ethernet.org/	Gigabit Ethernet Forum	Provides some technical and industry information about gigabit Ethernet.

Using the Companion CD-ROM

The companion CD-ROM contains the complete text of this book in a fully searchable, digital format. The PDF file contains a hyperlink to each of the RFCs and protocols discussed in the text. Just click on the link and access the RFC or protocol directly from the rfc-editor.org site.

What You Need

In order to use the CD-ROM, you'll need:

- IBM compatible running Windows 3.1 or better, or a Mac running OS 7.0 or better
- 16 MB RAM
- Web browser installed
- Internet connection
- Adobe Acrobat Reader 4.0
- 4MG of space on your hard drive (if you plan to install Adobe Acrobat Reader from the CD-ROM)

The Adobe Acrobat Reader 4.0 for 16 bit, 32 bit, and Mac operating systems are included on the CD-ROM in the Reader directory. To install it on your computer, open the subfolder for your operating system, and double click on the installation file.

Accessing the RFCs

The PDF file contains hyperlinks to the RFCs and Protocols discussed in the book. To access the text:

Double-click on the file email.pdf that is located in the root directory. This launches Adobe Acrobat Reader and opens the searchable version of the text. If you prefer, you can open email.pdf directly from the File menu in Adobe Acrobat Reader. Choose Open, and access your CD-ROM drive to browse for the email.pdf file.

Accessing the RFCs and protocols is easy. Just click on the hyperlink for the RFC or protocol you want to access. Adobe Acrobat will launch your Web browser and bring up the current version of the file you selected.

NOTE To take advantage of the hyperlink feature, you may need to configure Adobe Acrobat Reader to recognize your browser. If your browser does not launch when you click on a hyperlink:

1. In the File menu of Adobe Acrobat Reader, choose Preferences and select Weblink. The Weblink Preferences window appears.

2. In the textbox under Web Browser Application, enter the path to your browser. If you do not know the path, click the browse button to locate the application on your computer. Select the application file and click the OK button. The path is inserted into the text box.

3. Connection Type, select the name of your browser from the drop-down menu.

4. Click OK to save your selections.

User Assistance and Information

The software accompanying this book is being provided as is without warranty or support of any kind. Should you require basic installation assistance, or if your media is defective, please call our product support number at (212) 850-6194 weekdays between 9 am and 4 pm Eastern Standard Time. Or, we can be reached via e-mail at: wprtusw@wiley.com.

To place additional orders or to request information about other Wiley products, please call (800) 879-4539.

Index

To use this CD-ROM, your system must meet the following requirements:

Platform/Processor/Operating System. IBM compatible running Windows 3.1 or better; Mac running System 7.0 or better.

RAM. 16 MB

Hard Drive Space. 4 MG to install Adobe Acrobat Reader from the CD-ROM

Peripherals.

CD-ROM drive

Web browser installed

Adobe Acrobate Reader installed (provided on CD-ROM)

Internet Connection